Speak to the Bones

*How to Be a Prophetic People in a
Time of Exile*

Richard A. Brown

Isaac's Press
Blue Springs, Missouri

Also by Richard A. Brown
  What Was Paul Thinking? (2010)

Photo credit back cover: Marvin Crozier

Copyright © 2017 by Richard A. Brown
Isaac's Press is the registered imprint of Isaac's Press, LLC. Permission is granted to copy or reprint limited portions for noncommercial use, with attribution.

ISBN 978-0-9844815-2-1

Library of Congress Control Number: 2017900449
Library of Congress subject headings:
Religion & Philosophy
Christianity
Bible
Old Testament
New Testament
Hebrew Prophets
Apostle Paul

Version 1.1

"The hand of the LORD came upon me, and he brought me out by the spirit of the Lord and set me down in the middle of a valley; it was full of bones. He led me all around them; there were very many lying in the valley, and they were very dry.

"He said to me, 'Son of man, can these bones live?' I answered, 'O LORD God, you know.' Then he said to me, 'Prophesy to these bones, and say to them: O dry bones, hear the word of the Lord. Thus says the LORD God to these bones: I will cause breath to enter you, and you shall live....'"

—Ezekiel 37:1-4

Table of Contents

Introduction

Waking Up in Exile

Church pews are emptier these days, and the people still sitting in them tend to be older. Offering plates are lighter, too. As a result, congregations see no other choice but to reduce staff and cut back on programs and ministries. In our consumer-oriented, profit-driven culture, it's all about the numbers, after all.

Churches are measured and judged by the same standards as every other institution: **Market Share** (the size of the weekend crowd); **Income** (the money in the offering plate or from direct bank deposits); **Physical Presence** (the church building and its campus, often more shopping mall than sacred place); **Products and Services** (for others or just the members).

The downward spiral of this numbers game has ripple effects: Denominations downsize. Their publishing houses go out of business. Mission boards and seminaries respond to budget shortfalls with cutbacks. Land is sold. Unused buildings are repurposed or sometimes just left to rot and crumble.

Regular church attendance used to mean every Sunday morning, perhaps on Sunday and Wednesday evenings, as well. Now, it's just whenever people feel like going.

This used to be a problem faced just by Mainline Protestants. More recently it's spread to Southern Baptists and other evangelicals. It if weren't for massive Hispanic immigration, the Roman Catholic Church would be lumped in this category, too. Tragically, it carries the added burden of decades of sexual abuse of children by priests and other religious orders.

It's not surprising, then, that opinion polls reveal a shrinking percentage of the U. S. population identifies as Christian (although at 70-plus percent that's still a solid majority). The number of people checking the "none" box continues to grow, especially among younger folks. They're much more likely to self-describe as "spiritual but not religious." Older folks have begun to give that response, too. What's happening in the U.S. has already happened in Canada and Europe.

So, what's going on? Is Christianity dying in North America? Or has the death knell already sounded and we're just waiting for burial? If there *are* answers, are they religious, political, social, or generational? Is this about the institutions themselves or the spiritual nature of human beings these days? Have all the rules changed and nobody's told us yet?

As much as we'd all like to find a simple explanation, or at least a clear pathway through the maze, there probably isn't one. Clearly something major—and massive—is going on.

Eventually we may look back and, with hindsight, see it all clearly. In the meantime, for those of us who remain hopeful, we can draw on our faith and our imagination.

John Lennon did some imagining a few decades ago. The lyrics to his greatest solo hit—and one of the most cherished popular songs of our time—are worth noting:

Imagine there's no heaven
It's easy if you try
No hell below us
Above us only sky
Imagine all the people
Living for today

  Chorus:
You may say I'm a dreamer
But I'm not the only one
I hope someday you'll join us
And the world will be as one.

Imagine there's no countries
It isn't hard to do
Nothing to kill or die for
And no religion too
Imagine all the people
Living life in peace

Imagine no possessions
I wonder if you can
No need for greed or hunger
A brotherhood of man
Imagine all the people
Sharing all the world[1]

Some folks hear this message as anti-religion. Lennon himself refuted that in the last major interview he gave before his untimely death:

> If you can *imagine* a world at peace, with no denominations of religion—not without religion but without this my God-is-bigger-than-your-God thing—then it can be true ... the World Church [*sic*] called me once and asked, "Can we use the lyrics to 'Imagine' and just change it to 'Imagine *one* religion'?" That showed [me] they didn't understand it at all. It would defeat the whole purpose of the song, the whole idea. ²

A popular bumper sticker credits Mohandas Gandhi with this statement: "I like your Christ, I do not like your Christians. Your Christians are so unlike your Christ." Most likely, Gandhi never said those words, although it could be argued he probably wouldn't have disputed the thought.

Think of it this way: There is Christ. There are Christians. There is Christianity. And there is Christendom. Certainly, those terms are related but they're hardly the same thing.

Two thousand years after its founding, Christianity remains one of the world's great religions. It didn't start out that way, of course. First came the remembered words and acts of an itinerant Jewish rabbi/teacher from Galilee named Jesus. He was executed by the Romans, with an assist from the Jewish temple leaders. That should have meant an end to the small band of his followers. But something amazing united them after Jesus' crucifixion. They claimed he rose from his grave. That small community operated underground and, surprisingly, began to grow.

> ### *"There is Christ. There are Christians. There is Christianity. And there is Christendom. Certainly, those terms are related but they're hardly the same thing."*

Within a few years an educated Jew named Saul, whose Roman citizenship offered him easy access to the Greek-speaking world of the empire, began to establish communities of believers in Asia Minor and Greece. The letters he wrote, using his Greek name of Paul, circulated widely. The "Way of Jesus" was spreading, although still largely underground for fear of Roman reprisals.

By the end of that first century, writers we know as Mark, Matthew, Luke, and John (in that order) wrote accounts of Jesus' life—what he said and did. They weren't the kind of objective, journalistic accounts we'd expect today. Their purpose was to proclaim, to persuade, to explain, and to connect Jesus with the long-awaited Jewish Messiah (in Greek, "Christ"). Eventually the names Jesus and Christ became synonymous.

For three centuries the Way of Jesus existed as an underground movement in opposition to the empire. At the start of the fourth century, the Roman Emperor Constantine shrewdly made Christianity legal. He wanted their help to shore up his crumbling empire. Christians could now practice their faith openly.

It wasn't long before Christianity became an arm of the state. The emperor appointed and financially supported bishops, whose religious authority carried the weight of civil law. Bishops could force legal adherence to Christian beliefs and practices.

Historians can argue whether the empire co-opted Christianity or it was the other way around. Probably some of both. In any event, it marked the beginning of Christendom—the union of church and state, religion and politics.

This was more than 300 years *after* Jesus! Originally, the Way of Jesus that leads to God was a matter of community first, practices second, and belief as a result of the first two. That's how those first followers developed a vital faith. After all, Jesus didn't walk along the Sea of Galilee shouting to fishermen, "Have faith!" or "Accept these doctrines!"

"For three centuries the Way of Jesus existed as an underground movement in opposition to the empire."

No, he called out, "Follow me." When they did he gave them things to do, showing them how to accomplish those tasks. This involved healing, teaching, feeding, listening, and preaching side by side with them. Eventually, Jesus sent them out on their own. They returned amazed and energized. In short, their actions shaped their faith.

Compare that to the way most Christian churches operate now: first, beliefs (doctrines, creeds, rules) are taught. Appropriate behavior comes next, which lines up with those fixed belief statements. The end result is belonging to an organization that offers a way of life based on those beliefs and behaviors. Often there is a promised reward of a place in heaven after death. Conversely, those who stray will

> ## *"They survived because they knew who they were and whose they were. They were citizens of a kingdom other than Caesar's."*

be damned with eternal torment in hell. It's a tidy system that rewards obedience and punishes just about everything else.

Take a moment to consider just how far apart those two scenarios are.

The first followers of the Way lived on the margins of a society tightly controlled by the Romans. They had no political power, social standing, or economic might. They expressed their spiritual lives in the privacy of homes, often appearing in public to be little different from their secular neighbors. Still, like Jesus before them, they opposed the powerful and corrupt religious elite of the temple in Jerusalem.

Certainly, from the vantage point of both the Romans and the Jewish leadership, those believers were irrelevant and annoying. Yet within a few decades this underground movement spread beyond the Jewish homeland and into important urban outposts of the empire, even to Rome itself.

They survived because they knew *who* they were and *whose* they were. They were citizens of a kingdom other than Caesar's. In that sense, they fit the definition of exiles. To be an exile was and is part of the spiritual DNA of the Jews.

Judaism is about more than just remembering what happened to ancestors. Jews continue to retell and "re-participate" in the two central events of their history: *Exodus* from slavery in Egypt and *Exile* in Babylon.

God (Yahweh) rescued the descendants of Abraham and Sarah from political and cultural irrelevance. Within a few centuries they established the Kingdom of Israel in the land they believed was promised to Abraham's heirs. At its core was the theological idea that Israel was special to God.

"Prophets repeatedly warned them all of Yahweh's displeasure and predicted what would happen if their warnings went unheeded."

Yet a series of weak kings after David and Solomon led to splitting the kingdom into two smaller ones in the north (Israel) and south (Judah). There were good times and bad as major powers to their east and west rose and fell. That couldn't last forever.

First to fall was Israel, to Assyria. The obvious reason was that the Assyrian army was much more powerful, indeed the greatest superpower of the time. Beneath that, however, were other causes: arrogance, injustice, inequality, idolatry, selfishness, pride, and hubris. It would take a little longer before

Judah fell to the next superpower, Babylon, for pretty much all the same reasons.

It's not that the people and their leaders were blindsided by powerful enemy armies coming out of nowhere to bring chaos, destruction, and forced exile. Prophets repeatedly warned them all of Yahweh's displeasure and predicted what would happen if their warnings went unheeded.

A major portion of the Hebrew Bible (Christian Old Testament) includes a record of their prophetic utterances. Those prophets spoke from outside official channels and institutional roles, although there were a few exceptions to that rule.

The record of some of those prophets is found in what's known as the historical books (1 & 2 Kings, 1 & 2 Samuel, 1 & 2 Chronicles). The larger portion is located in books named for the rest: the three major prophets (so named because of the length of the books), Isaiah, Jeremiah, and Ezekiel; and twelve minor prophets (much shorter books, but certainly no less important than the others).

Most prophets came before the destruction of Israel and Judah, others during and after exile. By and large those prophets spoke truth to power from the margins of society. They criticized the community as a whole, but laid greater blame on the politically powerful and wealthy elite.

People who feel superior and exceptional often have a tough time dealing with change, much less their downfall and defeat. The exiled Jews cried by the waters of Babylon, taunted by their captors to "sing the songs of Zion." This led to one critical question: *"Lord, how could this be?"*

There was no quick-and-easy answer to that question, of course. It would take seventy years of captivity and the much-longer time of resettlement in their ancestral homeland to struggle with a way forward.

> *"By and large those prophets spoke truth to power from the margins of society. They criticized the community as a whole, but laid greater blame on the politically powerful and wealthy elite."*

In time the Jews began to shift the primary focus of their religion and spiritual life to a study of the written word. This required a new institution, the synagogue, to coexist alongside the rebuilt Jerusalem Temple. Rabbis taught and interpreted the law within the community while priests resumed ritual sacrifices in the temple.

After the Romans destroyed the temple in 70 CE, rabbis and synagogues remained alone at the core of Judaism. Ironically, this is how Judaism could survive being scattered throughout the empire, an event known as the Diaspora.

Prophets (at least ones within the scriptural tradition) no longer appeared within Judaism. New Testament letters, attributed to Paul and others, do list "prophet" as one of the many varieties of ministry within Christian community. However, the prophetic role did not become institutionalized as did priest, deacon, bishop, and elder. Still, this function appears to have played an important part in at least some of the varieties of Christian communities in the early-church period.

Richard Rohr, a Roman Catholic spirituality writer, notes that whenever the prophetic function is lacking in any group or religion, such a group will very soon be self-serving, self-maintaining, self-perpetuating, and self-promoting. When the prophets are kicked out of any group, it's a very short time until that group is circling the wagons around itself, and all sense of mission and message is lost. I am afraid this is the natural movement of any institution. Establishments of any kind usually move toward their own self-perpetuation, rather than "What are we doing for others?"[3]

Rohr goes on to explain the vital, if often unappreciated role played by prophets:

Prophets step in to disrupt the usual social consensus — "How wonderful our group is!" — and say, "It's just not entirely true!" So you see why the prophets are all killed (Matthew 23:29–39). Prophets expose and topple each group's idols and blind spots, very often showing that we make things into absolutes that are not absolutes in God's eyes, and we relativize what in fact is central and important. As Jesus so cleverly puts it, "You strain out gnats and you swallow camels" (Matthew 23:24).[4]

Something is emerging within Christianity in the early years of the 21st century. We're probably too close to it to fully understand its complexity. Nobody really knows exactly what the church will be like in even a few decades.

Some of those both within and outside Christianity contend the church is still tied to the idea of empire. This time, though, it's not the Roman empire but an American (or at least Western) one with capitalism and a military-industrial complex at its core.

"When the prophets are kicked out of any group, it's a very short time until that group is circling the wagons around itself, and all sense of mission and message is lost."

That is a hard and challenging critique on its own. The extent it has merit and, if so, to what degree, could take us in many directions. But our task here is to wonder what the church could become if we were to create a 21st-century version of the Way of Jesus. Now, this wouldn't require Christianity to become an illegal, subversive, underground movement as it basically was in its first three centuries. But it would lead to establishing communities of prophetic people who see their calling to move intentionally to the margins of the larger society.

Their purpose would begin with helping people (feeding the hungry, clothing the naked, housing the homeless, visiting the imprisoned, caring for the forgotten—to borrow the words Jesus quoted from Isaiah as he began his public ministry).

A prophetic people would take the next steps and address the larger, systemic causes of injustice, inequality, and idolatry. In doing so they would invite society's forgotten ones as equal partners in intentional communities where they feel safe, accepted, and valued.

Stories from the ancient Hebrew prophets can inspire, inform, and energize these communities of prophetic people. Fortunately, we have more ways to use scripture than the strict choice between biblical literalism and limiting the text to what it meant thousands of years ago.

Noted scholar Walter Brueggemann says a lot has changed in the last few decades.

> Interpreters no longer seek original intent of the text in the fashion of the late Supreme Court justice Antonin Scalia and as was demanded by historical criticism. Readers of scripture are no longer preoccupied with the author or the original context. Moreover, readers are aware that the biblical text cannot be corralled to serve any particular orthodoxy, which always required a somewhat skewed reading.[5]

Brueggemann goes on to say "scripture reading thrives on the generative force of imaginative interpretation." The result is to recognize that the interpretation of the biblical text (as well as its meaning) is complex. Typically, there is no single way to view or use the scripture text. Nor will it exist in a vacuum outside of the context in which it is used in its contemporary setting.

Sadly, our society today shares similarities with ancient Judah and Israel before, during, and after the Exile. Unlike them, though, our greatest need is not so much for individual prophets but whole communities led by the Holy Spirit and functioning in both prophetic and pastoral ways.

Their focus would be on the emerging reign of God in the present rather than on an after-death experience of heaven or hell. Such communities do not depend on the state to provide a theocratic system of government in which Christianity has most-favored status.

Instead, they would look for the Holy Spirit to lead them to where they might feel utterly unprepared and even afraid to go. That connection with the Spirit is essential and critical to the prophetic task.

The eight chapters that follow offer stories of ancient prophets who spoke truth to power. Readers may be surprised, fascinated, and sometimes even troubled by the details. Those prophets raised their voices against corruption, injustice, and a whole range of other human failings. Sometimes they succeeded; other times not so much (Nathan was able to change King David's mind, while John the Baptist ended up with his head literally on a platter presented to Herod Antipas).

It's important to keep in mind how much culture, religious practice, and understandings of God have changed over the past three or four thousand years. Add to that the fact that the stories recorded in the Bible were never meant to be objective, journalistic reporting. Nor can they provide a precise checklist of tasks to accomplish. But we can discern principles important to prophetic people living in intentional communities on the margins of society.

Translating those principles into action is the central purpose of this book.

Notes

1. Words and music by John Lennon, copyright 1971.
2. David Sheff. G. Barry Golson, ed., *All We Are Saying: The Last Major Interview with John*

Lennon and Yoko Ono (2000 ed.; first ed. 1981), St Martin's Griffin, 212-213.

3. Comments appeared in the blog, "Richard Rohr's Daily Meditation" (Copyright © 2015 Center for Action and Contemplation), adapted from *Way of the Prophet* (no longer available) and *Prophets Then, Prophets Now* (CD, MP3 download).

4. Ibid.

5. Walter Brueggemann, in a book review of *Uses and Abuses of Moses* by Theodore Ziolkowski, in *The Christian Century* 133, no. 21 (October 12, 2016): 54.

For Reflection & Discussion

1. How fair is it to measure and judge churches by consumer-oriented categories such as market share, income, physical presence, and products and services? Are there other, more appropriate ways to do this?

2. Describe in a few sentences what you think is happening to the Christian church in North America? What changes have you observed in your lifetime?

3. Why do you think John Lennon's classic song, "Imagine," has remained popular for so many decades? What is the core message in the lyrics? Which phrases in particular speak to you? If none do, why not?

4. What do the following related terms mean: Way of Jesus, Christianity, Christendom? How are they different from one another?

5. The author contends the original Way of Jesus was a matter of first belonging to community, then engaging in religious/spiritual practices, and finally accepting beliefs and doctrines. This

compares to the path of many Christian communities today: first accepting doctrines and beliefs, then aligning personal behavior to those beliefs, and finally belonging to an organization. How much do you agree with this assessment? What does each path say about believers and institutions?

6. What were some of the roles played by Hebrew prophets in ancient Israel and Judah, before and after the Babylonian exile?

7. Discuss Richard Rohr's comment that "whenever the prophetic function is lacking in any group or religion, such a group will very soon be self-serving, self-maintaining, self-perpetuating, and self-promoting."

8. How familiar are you with stories of the prophets in the Old Testament? Why is that the case?

9. Walter Brueggemann is quoted as saying that "scripture reading thrives on the generative force of imaginative interpretation." What do you think this means? Why do you think it might be important to view scripture in the context in which it is used today?

10. How do you understand the process of the emerging reign/kingdom of God on earth as it is in heaven?

11. What's the difference between developing a precise checklist of prophetic tasks to accomplish and discerning principles important to prophetic people living in intentional communities on the margins of society?

12. What do you hope to learn from this book?

Chapter 1
Nathan: Speaking Truth to Power

It was a moment—no, *the* moment—that not only stopped a popular, beloved, and powerful king in his tracks but that also set the pattern for practically every other prophet in Israel's history: *"You are that man!"*

Kings in the ancient Mideast didn't have to listen to religious leaders. In almost every case kings (and in rare circumstances, queens) *were* the chief religious leaders. Most even considered themselves deities or at least a "son of the gods." Therefore, anybody who dared to confront a king with a version of the truth different from the official one wouldn't be around to talk about it for long. That was not the case, however, with the prophet Nathan and Israel's King David.

This particular tale of lust, adultery, and secretly arranged murder travels well across the centuries. It sounds as right at home in the 21st century CE as it was in the 9th century BCE. (David was born in 907 BCE and died in 837 BCE after a 40-year reign.)

The story of David and Bathsheba remains one of the best known tales in the entire Bible. This is true, primarily of course, because of its sexual content.

But what it reveals about the role of Israelite prophets may be a far more important matter.

The whole story is presented in 2 Samuel chapter 11, and it's certainly worth spending some time to learn all the details. Let's just cover the highlights here.

King David was already married, to the daughter of his predecessor. King Saul had turned out to be a failure militarily and religiously, a fact credited to the removal of divine blessing. After a great deal of civil strife, David ended up as king. He established Jerusalem as his capital, with his palace, naturally, as the biggest, tallest, and best house in the whole city.

One evening he was out on the roof of his house and looked down onto the roof of a neighboring building. That's where a strikingly beautiful woman named Bathsheba was relaxing after bathing. She was the wife of a Hittite named Uriah, one of the king's military commanders who happened to be out of town at the time on a military campaign.

> *"This particular tale of lust, adultery, and secretly arranged murder travels well across the centuries. It sounds as right at home in the 21st century CE as it was in the 9th century BCE."*

King David was smitten by Bathsheba's beauty and sent one of his servants to her house to bring her to the palace. Long story short: Bathsheba and

David began an adulterous affair which, sometime later on, resulted in a pregnancy. And so David concocted a cover story: He orders Uriah home from the battlefield, expecting him to spend some time with his wife. That way he would think Bathsheba's baby was his. No such luck.

Out of a sense of duty to king and his fellow soldiers, Uriah refused to indulge in the pleasures of home life and actually camped out with fellow soldiers outside David's palace.

David then devised a Plan B: He has Uriah sent back into battle. Secretly he also orders Uriah's commanding officer to put him in the most dangerous part of the battle before having his comrades fall back, thus exposing Uriah to certain death. Plan B works like a charm.

When Bathsheba got the news of her husband's death she began a time of mourning. But when the official mourning period ended, David invited her to the palace, where she soon became his wife. A few months later she bore him a son.

Normally, this would be just one more example of "What the king wants, the king gets." But this was in Israel, which operated by different rules. Let's pick up the narrative provided by the writer of 2 Samuel:

> But the thing that David had done displeased the Lord, and the Lord sent Nathan to David. He came to him, and said to him, "There were two men in a certain city, the one rich and the other poor. The rich man had very many flocks and herds; but the poor man had nothing but one little ewe lamb, which he had bought. He brought it up, and it grew up with him and with his children; it used to eat of his meager fare,

25

and drink from his cup, and lie in his
bosom, and it was like a daughter to him.

Now there came a traveler to the rich
man, and he was loath to take one of his
own flock or herd to prepare for the
wayfarer who had come to him, but he took
the poor man's lamb, and prepared that for
the guest who had come to him."

Then David's anger was greatly kindled
against the man. He said to Nathan, "As the
Lord lives, the man who has done this
deserves to die; he shall restore the lamb
fourfold, because he did this thing, and
because he had no pity."

Nathan said to David, "You are the man!
Thus says the Lord, the god of Israel: I
anointed you king over Israel, and I rescued
you from the hand of Saul; I gave you your
master's house, and your master's wives
into your bosom, and gave you the house of
Israel and of Judah; and if that had been too
little, I would have added as much more.

"Why have you despised the word of the
Lord, to do what is evil in his sight? You
have struck down Uriah the Hittite with the
sword, and have taken his wife to be your
wife, and have killed him with the sword of
the Ammonites. Now therefore the sword
shall never depart from your house, for you
have despised me, and have taken the wife
of Uriah the Hittite to be your wife. Thus
says the Lord: I will raise up trouble against
you from within your own house; and I will
take your wives before your eyes, and give
them to your neighbor, and he shall lie with
your wives in the sight of this very sun. For

26

you did it secretly; but I will do this thing before all Israel, and before the sun."

David said to Nathan. "I have sinned against the Lord." Nathan said to David, "Now the Lord has put away your sin; you shall not die. Nevertheless, because by this deed you have utterly scorned the Lord: the child that is born to you shall die." Then Nathan went to his house.

—2 Samuel 12:1-15

Twenty-first-century readers tend to go straight to the sexual component of this sordid tale. There are a couple other aspects worth mentioning, however. Notice how Nathan appeals to David's sense of rightness by telling a story of a rich man who steals the property of a poor man, rather than a story just about lust and adultery.

In the ancient world a man's wife was considered his property, in much the same manner as his household possessions and livestock. Therefore, the prophet spoke within the patriarchal culture of his time: stealing a lamb and stealing a wife were roughly comparable actions. This would be appalling in our day but made perfect sense in Nathan and David's.

"In the ancient world a man's wife was considered his property, in much the same manner as his household possessions and livestock."

Add to this the simple factor of economic disparity and injustice. The rich man has no right to take the property of the poor man. In Nathan's story the rich man appears to have no such qualms. David, however, apparently accepted a different standard of moral conduct.

Nathan was not the first person to speak truth to power. But his courageous act broke ground for later prophets to confront kings, queens, priests, and society's wealthy elites for their acts of injustice and idolatry. Just about anywhere else, religious figures who dared to speak and act in this way were executed.

That's not to say the leaders of Israel and Judah always listened to and respected the prophets. Here among the Israelites, however, the power of royalty, priestly hierarchy, and wealth was not to be the final authority. That belonged to the word of God, and prophets bore the often unenviable task of speaking it aloud.

David's act of repentance — *"I have sinned against the Lord"* — saved his life. Sadly, the son born as a result of his and Bathsheba's adultery died. But another son born to the couple would eventually succeed David on Israel's throne. Solomon would accomplish far more than his father ever dreamed.

> **David's act of repentance, "I have sinned against the Lord," saved his life. Sadly, the son born as a result of his and Bathsheba's adultery died.**

Interestingly, it was Nathan who put an end to one of David's chief dreams: to build a temple in Jerusalem as a resting place for the ark of the covenant. And at the end of David's life Nathan, along with the priest Zadok, supported Solomon's rise to power, even though he was not the eldest of David's sons.

How and why David was prohibited from building the temple in Jerusalem offers us an interesting story in its own right:

> Now when the king was settled in his house, and the Lord had given him rest from all his enemies around him, the king said to the prophet Nathan, "See now, I am living in a house of cedar, but the ark of God stays in a tent." Nathan said to the king, "Go, do all that you have in mind; for the Lord is with you."
>
> But that same night the word of the Lord came to Nathan: Go and tell my servant David: Thus says the Lord: Are you the one to build me a house to live in? I have not lived in a house since the day I brought up the people of Israel from Egypt to this day, but I have been moving about in a tent and a tabernacle.
>
> Wherever I have moved about among all the people of Israel, did I ever speak a word with any of the tribal leaders of Israel, whom I commanded to shepherd my people Israel, saying, "Why have you not built me a house of cedar?"
>
> Now therefore thus you shall say to my servant David: "Thus says the Lord of hosts: I took you from the pasture, from following the sheep to be prince over my people Israel; and I have been with you wherever you went, and have cut off all your enemies

from before you; and I will make for you a great name, like the name of the great ones

"Your house and your kingdom shall be made sure forever before me; your throne shall be established forever."

of the earth. And I will appoint a place for my people Israel and will plant them, so that they may live in their own place, and be disturbed no more; and evildoers shall afflict them no more, as formerly, from the time that I appointed judges over my people Israel; and I will give you rest from all your enemies.

Moreover the Lord declares to you that the Lord will make you a house. When your days are fulfilled and you lie down with your ancestors, I will raise up your offspring after you, who shall come forth from your body, and I will establish his kingdom.

He shall build a house for my name, and I will establish the throne of his kingdom forever. I will be a father to him, and he shall be a son to me. When he commits iniquity, I will punish him with a rod such as mortals use, with blows inflicted by human beings.

But I will not take my steadfast love from him, as I took it from Saul, whom I put away from before you. Your house and your kingdom shall be made sure forever before me; your throne shall be established forever. In accordance with all these words

and with all this vision, Nathan spoke to
David. –2 Samuel 7:1-17

The writers of the historical books offer slightly
different interpretations as to why David was prohibited from building the temple in Jerusalem (see
also 1 Chronicles 17; 1 Chronicles 28:1–3, 6; and 1
Kings 5:3). Both before and during David's reign he
had been a "man of war," and thus it would be
inappropriate for him to build a house for God. His
son and successor, however, would be known as a
"man of peace," and that was a whole different
matter.

David assembled at Jerusalem all the
officials of Israel, the officials of the tribes,
the officers of the divisions that served the
king, the commanders of the thousands, the
commanders of the hundreds, the stewards
of all the property and cattle of the king and
his sons, together with the palace officials,
the mighty warriors, and all the warriors.
Then King David rose to his feet and
said: "Hear me, my brothers and my people.
I had planned to build a house of rest for
the ark of the covenant of the Lord, for the
footstool of our God; and I made
preparations for building.
But God said to me, 'You shall not build a
house for my name, for you are a warrior
and have shed blood.'... And of all my sons,
for the Lord has given me many, he has
chosen my son Solomon to sit upon the
throne of the kingdom of the Lord over
Israel. He said to me, 'It is your son
Solomon who shall build my house and my

courts, for I have chosen him to be a son to
me, and I will be a father to him.'"
                              —1 Chronicles 28:1–4, 6

Remember, too, Nathan's words to David when
confronting him over the affair with Bathsheba:

"You have struck down Uriah the Hittite
with the sword, and have taken his wife to
be your wife, and have killed him with the
sword of the Ammonites. Now therefore the
sword shall never depart from your house,
for you have despised me, and have taken
the wife of Uriah the Hittite to be your
wife."

Solomon offered a slightly different rationale in a
letter to King Hiram of Tyre, a longtime friend of his
father's. This appears to lessen David's actions as a
"man of war," which was necessary because of the
constant warring of neighboring city-states:

Now King Hiram of Tyre sent his servants
to Solomon, when he heard that they had
anointed him king in place of his father; for
Hiram had always been a friend to David.
Solomon sent word to Hiram, saying, "You
know that my father David could not build a
house for the name of the Lord his God
because of the warfare with which his
enemies surrounded him, until the Lord put
them under the soles of his feet.
    But now the Lord my God has given me
rest on every side; there is neither adversary
nor misfortune. So I intend to build a house
for the name of the Lord my God, as the

Lord said to my father David, `Your son,
whom I will set on your throne in your
place, shall build the house for my name.'"
—1 Kings 5:1-5

King Hiram went on to play a key role in the
building of the temple. He provided much of the
building materials, including cedar wood from
Lebanon, as well as many of the skilled artisans.

We tend to forget, though, that Solomon
conscripted thousands of laborers (many of them
virtual slaves from foreign territories) and levied
heavy taxes on the people of his growing empire
during the years-long building process. If nothing
else, this ought to temper his well-known reputation
as a "man of peace."

David was not without divinely bestowed reward,
of course. Although he would not be permitted to
build a house of cedar for God (Yahweh), Nathan
promised something else from God: *"...the Lord
declares to you that the Lord will make you a
house.... Your house and your kingdom shall be
made sure forever before me; your throne shall be
established forever."*

This covenant with the house of David would
become as important to later generations in Judah
as the covenant Yahweh established on Mount Sinai
through Moses. That older covenant would be
emphasized over the Davidic one in the northern
Kingdom of Israel (one of the reasons the empire
was eventually split in two).

Unfortunately, they would misunderstand how
divine covenants work, believing divine protection
would come no matter what they did, or at the very
least, by the mere act of performing outward rituals
and sacrifices. That made their humiliating defeat,

the destruction of Jerusalem and its magnificent temple, and forced exile in Babylon all the more bewildering.

For Reflection & Discussion

1. Imagine you are the prophet Nathan and have become aware of the details surrounding David and Bathsheba. What thoughts run through your mind? Where would you begin to confront David? Why would it be important to stand up to the king?

2. David's act of repentance — *"I have sinned against the Lord"*—provided a turning point in this story. How did that affect not only David's subsequent life and reign but the history of the nation, as well? What is your own experience with the power of repentance? Is it the overwhelming factor involved or one of many in a chain of events?

3. How might the David and Bathsheba incident have empowered Nathan later on when David declared his intention to build a temple in Jerusalem?

4. Why did David become known as a "man of war," while his son Solomon is remembered as a "man of peace"? Discuss the fact that the latter's given name at birth was not Solomon but was changed because the new name is a variant of the Hebrew word *shalom*?

5. Share some contemporary examples of individuals and groups who have spoken truth to power. How did they end up? What was accomplished? Why might the struggles involved have been important?

6. Everyone's life carries positive and negative aspects. Make lists of those for David and Solomon. Which ones do we remember 2,500 years later? Why do you think that is so?
7. In your own words, explain the difference between a contract and a covenant.

Chapter 2

Elijah and the Voice of God

This was Elijah's moment. A massive crowd of Israelites waited for the spectacle to get underway: Elijah against 850 priests; Yahweh versus Baal, the Phoenician fertility god (and his female consort Asherah). King Ahab gathered them all on Mount Carmel. No doubt Jezebel, his Phoenician-born queen, was watching closely.

She and Elijah had locked horns for years as she promoted Baal worship in Israel (the northern half, along with Judah in the south, of David and Solomon's once united kingdom). She'd succeeded in converting the wealthy elite; not so much the lower classes.

Israel continued to be devastated by a drought that Elijah had prophesied three years before as punishment for his countrymen's lukewarm worship of Yahweh, their ancestral God. That was the setting as Elijah stepped forward:

> "'How long will you go limping with two
> different opinions? If the Lord is God,
> follow him; but if Baal, then follow him.'
> The people did not answer him a word.
> Then Elijah said to the people, 'I, even I

only, am left a prophet of the Lord; but Baal's prophets number four hundred fifty [*the other 400 were devotees of Asherah*]. Let two bulls be given to us; let them choose one bull for themselves, cut it in pieces, and lay it on the wood, but put no fire to it; I will prepare the other bull and lay it on the wood, but put no fire to it. Then you call on the name of your god and I will call on the name of the Lord; the god who answers by fire is indeed God." All the people answered, 'Well spoken!' Then Elijah said to the prophets of Baal, 'Choose for yourselves one bull and prepare it first, for you are many; then call on the name of your god, but put no fire to it.'" —1 Kings 18:21–25

> ***"'How long will you go limping with two different opinions? If the Lord is God, follow him; but if Baal, then follow him.' The people did not answer him a word."***

The priests of Baal slaughtered their bull. Then Elijah slaughtered his—all by himself! The priests hauled their bull up onto a pile of timber. All that was needed was lightning to set the sacrifice ablaze. Keep in mind that Israel hadn't had any rain for three years, so a sudden thunderstorm would be pretty persuasive, would it not?

As if all this wasn't quite enough of a spectacle, Elijah taunted his opponents. Perhaps if they all danced and hollered Baal would respond to their pleas.

"At noon Elijah mocked them, saying, 'Cry aloud! Surely he is a god; either he is meditating, or he has wandered away, or he is on a journey, or perhaps he is asleep and must be awakened.' Then they cried aloud and, as was their custom, they cut themselves with swords and lances until the blood gushed out over them. As midday passed, they raved on until the time of the offering of the oblation, but there was no voice, no answer, and no response."
—vss. 27–29

Elijah invited the crowd to come closer. Then he reconstructed an old altar on the site that Baal worshipers previously had wrecked.

"Elijah took twelve stones, according to the number of the tribes of the sons of Jacob, to whom the word of the Lord came, saying, 'Israel shall be your name'; with the stones he built an altar in the name of the Lord. Then he made a trench around the altar, large enough to contain two measures of seed. Next he put the wood in order, cut the bull in pieces, and laid it on the wood.

He said, 'Fill four jars with water and pour it on the burnt offering and on the wood.' Then he said, 'Do it a second time'; and they did it a second time. Again he said, 'Do it a third time'; and they did it a third time, so that the water ran all around the altar, and filled the trench also with water.

At the time of the offering of the oblation, the prophet Elijah came near and said, 'O Lord, God of Abraham, Isaac, and Israel, let

it be known this day that you are God in
Israel, that I am your servant, and that I
have done all these things at your bidding.
Answer me, O Lord, answer me, so that this
people may know that you, O Lord, are God,
and that you have turned their hearts back.'
Then the fire of the Lord fell and
consumed the burnt offering, the wood, the
stones, and the dust, and even licked up the
water that was in the trench. When all the
people saw it, they fell on their faces and
said, 'The Lord indeed is God; the Lord
indeed is God.'" —vss. 31–39

That's a pretty good story. No, that's a *great*
story. Setting aside the miraculous parts, it's still
loaded with biblical lessons: Yahweh's power is
greater than anyone or anything else. Yahweh had
not forsaken the people of Israel and had "turned
their hearts back." The people, in response, once
again publicly worshiped the God of their ancestors
Abraham, Isaac, and Jacob.

But that wasn't quite the end of the story. There
were three more parts to it—another uplifting,
miraculous event sandwiched between two
troubling details. The first challenging aspect:

"Elijah said to them, 'Seize the prophets of
Baal; do not let one of them escape.' Then
they seized them; and Elijah brought them
down to the Wadi Kishon, and killed them
there." —vs. 40

**Elijah personally slaughters hundreds of
human beings! Just let that sink in.**

40

How can this possibly be considered appropriate behavior, particularly by one of God's chosen prophets? Elijah's mass homicide would not go unchallenged, though, but first the prophet and King Ahab would meet face to face. Remember that the whole reason for the contest on Mount Carmel was a multi-year drought. Neither the miraculous lightning bolt that consumed Elijah's altar nor the killing of the priests ended that.

> "Elijah said to Ahab, 'Go up, eat and drink; for there is a sound of rushing rain.' So Ahab went up to eat and to drink. Elijah went up to the top of Carmel; there he bowed himself down upon the earth and put his face between his knees. He said to his servant, 'Go up now, look toward the sea.' He went up and looked, and said, 'There is nothing.' Then he said, 'Go again seven times.' At the seventh time he said, 'Look, a little cloud no bigger than a person's hand is rising out of the sea.'
> Then he said, 'Go say to Ahab, "Harness your chariot and go down before the rain stops you."' In a little while the heavens grew black with clouds and wind; there was a heavy rain. Ahab rode off and went to Jezreel. But the hand of the Lord was on Elijah; he girded up his loins and ran in front of Ahab to the entrance of Jezreel."
> —vss. 41–46

Now, the beginning of the third act:

> "Ahab told Jezebel all that Elijah had done, and how he had killed all the prophets with

41

the sword. Then Jezebel sent a messenger to Elijah, saying, 'So may the gods do to me, and more also, if I do not make your life like the life of one of them by this time tomorrow.' Then he was afraid; he got up and fled for his life, and came to Beer-sheba, which belongs to Judah; he left his servant there.

But he himself went a day's journey into the wilderness, and came and sat down under a solitary broom tree. He asked that he might die: `It is enough; now, O Lord, take away my life, for I am no better than my ancestors.' Then he lay down under the broom tree and fell asleep."

—1 Kings 19:1-5a

This had been quite the adventure for Elijah. First the big contest on Mount Carmel in which Yahweh's power overwhelmed the priests of Baal and Asherah. Then the slaughter of those 450 priests, followed by the return of rain to Israel, thus ending a lengthy drought. This, in turn, led to Queen Jezebel's death threat and the prophet's flight into the desert. All was lost, Elijah thought. And so he begged God to take his life. Defeated and without hope he lay down under a tree to wait for death to come.

"All was lost, Elijah thought. And so he begged God to take his life."

Let's pause here. It's as good a time as any to consider the violence running through this entire story. This is, after all, God's "chosen one" who murders 450 people. Apparently, this horrendous act is just fine with God!

42

Now if this were an isolated act it might be explained away somehow or possibly even overlooked. *But it's not.*

Violence connected indirectly or directly with God—often brutal and on a massive scale—is found throughout the Old Testament. It's there in post-creation accounts, throughout the history of the patriarchs, the Hebrews' captivity in Egypt and eventual exodus, in the conquest and settlement of Canaan (their promised land), and repeatedly in the history of Israel and its eventual destruction and forced exile.

How do we Christians deal with that? It's impossible to read the Old Testament and *not* notice (a) the barbaric acts committed by human beings in God's name that are apparently made legitimate by God and (b) violent acts perpetrated directly by God. On the other hand, we have God's "good news" of love, grace, forgiveness, and rebirth evident in the person, ministry, and mission of Jesus Christ. What gives?

The easy answer would be that the New Testament gospel of Christ replaced the Old Testament rule of law (theologians use the term "superseded"). But it's a very short step from that position to rejecting the Old Testament as holy scripture.

From there it's another short jump to the mistaken idea that God replaced the Jews with Christians, making them the "*new* Israel," or favored family of God, at the expense of "*old* Israel." And while many Christians over the centuries have taken that tragic, mistaken turn, it's the wrong path entirely.

We might be justified in understanding some Old Testament violence as metaphor or allegory rather than literal truth. For example, consider the way the

Hebrew tribes settled Canaan forty years after their exodus from Egypt. We could read this as a story of liberation for a formerly oppressed people rather than as a triumphant account of conquest by a powerful military force fulfilling a divine mandate.

The primary lesson here would be that the Hebrew tribes needed to learn total dependence on and devotion to God rather than nationalistic arrogance and cruel vindictiveness.

"Can true peace and justice ever result from murder and mayhem?"

It's also possible to view this supposedly God-sanctioned violence by prophets such as Elijah as a divine corrective to human violence—sort of an "ends justifying the means" process. This could make it part of a larger picture: God's desire for justice for the poor and oppressed as well as a corrective to idolatry. But can true peace and justice *ever* result from murder and mayhem?

Walter Brueggemann, one of Christianity's foremost scholars on Old Testament themes and theology, expressed his unease with these approaches:

> The first cause of my disquiet is that this trajectory of interpretation never takes the voicing of divine violence as serious revealed data about the character of God. But what if God is disclosed in the text as an agent of violence? What if this God has a propensity toward violence with which God struggles, as in Hosea 11:1–9? What if God's own life is unsettled and in contestation?

44

What if we are made in the image of a God who struggles with violence? I think we are required to struggle with such questions, not to explain away violence in scripture.[1]

Brueggemann goes on:

The second, more practical reason for my disquiet is that when the question of violence is posed by serious readers of the Bible, this response of explaining away is not adequate or persuasive. I think we are...trapped in an interpretive practice that refuses to struggle with the deep complexity of the character of God. The question is exceedingly hard, and easy answers will not suffice. But the relentless rhetoric remains! If we dared to read such texts in church, we more than likely would still blithely respond, "Thanks be to God." We have much more hard work to do.[2]

Some of that hard work will include looking carefully at the biblical theme of power/strength versus vulnerability/innocence. Christians celebrate the beginnings of God's kingdom or reign on earth with the birth of a baby to an unmarried couple, marginalized by their society, in an out-of-the-way corner of the Roman empire.

That child would grow up to teach that the greatest among us is one who chooses servanthood over prestige and position. His eventual death, executed on a cross by the method reserved for the worst of criminals, would lead to the greatest exhibition of divine power in all history: the resurrection we continue to celebrate each Easter.

Strength and weakness. Power and abandon-
ment. Brutality and loving-kindness. These are all
issues that Christians must struggle with at some
point. They are all there in the Bible—in both
testaments. Their presence cannot be ignored or
glossed over. Why would the ancient writers of the
Bible make direct connections between brutal
violence and God's character and activity?

Is the key to this question to be found in the
nature of God or the limited understanding of
human beings? In any event, the Bible becomes
much more than the simple stories we probably
learned as children in Sunday school.

> *"Strength and weakness.*
> *Power and abandonment.*
> *Brutality and loving-kindness.*
> *These are all issues that*
> *Christians must struggle with*
> *at some point."*

Elijah's story does not end under a desert broom
tree. The way the biblical writer spins this tale gives
us some insight into the nature of prophetic ministry and also offers a helpful glimpse into the character and ways of God:

> [Elijah] asked that he might die: "It is
> enough; now, O Lord, take away my life, for
> I am no better than my ancestors." Then he
> lay down under the broom tree and fell
> asleep. Suddenly an angel touched him and
> said to him, "Get up and eat." He looked,
> and there at his head was a cake baked on
> hot stones, and a jar of water. He ate and

46

drank, and lay down again. The angel of the
Lord came a second time, touched him, and
said, "Get up and eat, otherwise the journey
will be too much for you." He got up, and
ate and drank; then he went in the strength
of that food forty days and forty nights to
Horeb the mount of God. At that place he
came to a cave, and spent the night there.
—1 Kings 19:4–9

The prophet's journey and task required strength
and stamina. And so Elijah heeded an angel's direction to eat and drink, followed by rest, then more
eating and drinking. After a forty-day journey he hid
in a cave, on the same mountain where centuries
before Moses received the law from God.

Then the word of the Lord came to him,
saying, "What are you doing here, Elijah?"
He answered, "I have been very zealous for
the Lord, the God of hosts; for the Israelites
have forsaken your covenant, thrown down
your altars, and killed your prophets with
the sword. I alone am left, and they are
seeking my life, to take it away." He said,
"Go out and stand on the mountain before
the Lord, for the Lord is about to pass by."
Now there was a great wind, so strong
that it was splitting mountains and breaking
rocks in pieces before the Lord, but the Lord
was not in the wind; and after the wind an
earthquake, but the Lord was not in the
earthquake; and after the earthquake a fire,
but the Lord was not in the fire; and after
the fire a sound of sheer silence. When
Elijah heard it, he wrapped his face in his

mantle and went out and stood at the entrance of the cave.

Then there came a voice to him that said, "What are you doing here, Elijah?" He answered, "I have been very zealous for the Lord, the God of hosts; for the Israelites have forsaken your covenant, thrown down your altars, and killed your prophets with the sword. I alone am left, and they are seeking my life, to take it away."

—vss. 9b–14

Fleeing for 40 days and nights is the biblical way of saying Elijah ran for as far and as long as humanly possible. He probably thought he was safe from both Jezebel and God. But in a cave tucked into a mountainside, he heard a voice that was already there waiting for him: *What are you doing here, Elijah?* Forty days before he had given up, recognizing the hopelessness of his situation. But now God calmed him down so he could focus on what was truly important about his ministry and mission.

> **"Fleeing for 40 days and nights is the biblical way of saying Elijah ran for as far and as long as humanly possible. He probably thought he was safe from both Jezebel and God."**

No doubt Elijah still remembered the big show back on Mount Carmel. Could that possibly have been a more impressive exhibition of divine power? *No.* Elijah was now to learn there's more to God than spectacle. And so he was told to stand at the cave's entrance as one overwhelming display of nature's power after another passed by: wind, earthquake, and fire. But the Lord was not in the wind or the earthquake or the fire. In the end there was just silence and a voice whispering to him: *"What are you doing here, Elijah?"*

It's perhaps human nature to compare God's power and presence to natural events or human spectacles. But God is greater than wind and earthquake and fire—and dramatic, miraculous demonstrations before massive audiences.

> *"We will wonder what it means that we are made in God's image and called to participate in establishing God's kingdom on earth as it is in heaven."*

Maybe Walter Brueggemann is correct in wondering if God struggles with a propensity for violence. We can't know that for sure, of course. Or is it a typically human thing to explain our own propensity for violence by transferring it onto God?

Wrestling with these kinds of questions can expand our concept of God. In turn, we will wonder what it means that we are made in God's image and called to participate in establishing God's kingdom on earth as it is in heaven.

There's much more to Elijah's story than Mount Carmel and the mountainside cave. His long life of prophetic ministry was filled with preaching ("telling forth" divine truths) and healing and faithfulness.

He faced physical and spiritual challenges. He showed courage and fear, boldness and resignation. Through it all, God kept calling him back into the arena where God's people needed his ministry.

Furthermore, the Elijah stories are a challenge first to Jews who live on *this* side of the Babylonian Exile. The eventual destruction of the Jerusalem Temple by the Romans was a critical moment in the ongoing transformation of Judaism itself.

From beginning to end the Old Testament offers enormous changes in the ways that the nature, character, and activity of God are understood. The Genesis stories from creation through the patriarchs (Abraham, Isaac, Jacob, and Joseph) offer us a deity who is at first unknown but who gradually becomes identified with a particular tribe of nomads who eventually settle down in Canaan.

This Hebrew tribal god is often capricious and vengeful. From Israel's perspective that's a good thing: they are protected, delivered from Egyptian slavery, fed in the wilderness, and granted success in one battle after another. But from the perspective of Israel's enemies (whether they be Egypt or the Canaanites), this tribal god is cruel and blood-thirsty.

By the time of the divided kingdoms (Israel in the north and Judah in the south) this understanding of "God" still held sway. The people believed God would protect them from their enemies, no matter what—isn't that what "covenant" was all about, after all? Eventually, though, the Assyrian army conquered the northern kingdom, dispersing its people so thoroughly that today we refer to them as "the lost tribes of Israel."

Decades later Judah and its royal capital of Jerusalem fell to the Babylonians. True, some of those exiles' descendants eventually would "return home" from Babylon by order of the Persian king, Cyrus. But they would be subjects of the Persians, the Greeks, and finally the Romans.

> *"This Hebrew tribal god is often capricious and vengeful. From Israel's perspective that's a good thing.... But from the perspective of Israel's enemies ... this tribal god is cruel and bloodthirsty."*

Their image of God changed drastically after the exile. The volatile, vicious protector of Elijah would come to be known as One who acts primarily out of justice, compassion, and steadfast love. The earliest Christians continued this understanding, albeit within an ancient, pre-scientific worldview.

Two thousand years later Christians in the Western, industrialized, modern, and postmodern world face a task just as daunting as that faced by post-exilic Jews. The God of Elijah appears to us as foreign if not unrecognizable. We know that God does not cause tornadoes, earthquakes, and wildfires as either punishment or to prove God's existence.

But like Elijah we can experience God in the stillness, the silence, asking us the same question: *What are you doing here?*

Notes

1. Walter Brueggemenn, in a *Christian Century* review of fellow scholar Jerome F. D. Creach's book, *Violence in Scripture* (December 11, 2013).
2. Ibid.

For Reflection & Discussion

1. The biblical stories of the prophet Elijah are filled with dramatic spectacles, incredible miracles, and considerable violence. In what ways do those elements make these stories harder or easier to relate to readers in the 21st Century CE? How does it alter our appreciation for them if we accept that these accounts were never meant to be objective reporting?
2. Elijah's confrontation with hundreds of priests devoted to Baal and Asherah was pretty spectacular. In the end, though, what did it prove? What happened as a result of this public drama?
3. In what ways did King Ahab's foreign–born queen, Jezebel, play such a critical role in Elijah's life and ministry? What might this tell us about the biblical writers' intent regarding the influence of "foreigners" among the people of Israel? How has the "us versus them" theme appeared elsewhere in the Bible, in both Old and New Testaments? Why do you think outsiders are typically viewed as the bad guys? How did Jesus' parable of the good Samaritan upend this idea?

4. Describe the often-violent image of God in these biblical passages? How much might they reflect the character of God and/or the character of the people who worshiped Yahweh? Many people have trouble reconciling a "vengeful, murderous" God with a "loving Creator" God, both of which can be found in the Old Testament (Hebrew Bible). How have Christians handled this topic over the centuries?

5. All successful kingdoms/empires established by human beings have been built and maintained on the concept of "peace through victory," an approach characterized by violence, brutality, and rigid hierarchical power. Yet God's promised kingdom/empire is just the opposite: ultimate victory through nonviolent peace. Which elements of Elijah's story can help us deal with these divergent means and ends?

6. Review the story of Elijah in the mountainside cave. What are the key elements and lasting truths you derive? When have you, much like Elijah, experienced God in the stillness, the silence, asking the same question: *What are you doing here?* What happened next?

Chapter 3

Amos: Injustice and Judgment

Long before he became a prophet, Amos was a shepherd.

Most Bible readers probably wouldn't find anything unusual about that. After all, God appears to have a special connection with shepherds:

- Abel, son of Adam, was a shepherd who "found favor with God" (Genesis 4)
- Abraham is described as a chieftain with many herds of sheep (Genesis 21)
- Jacob was a shepherd for his Uncle Laban (Genesis 30)
- Joseph was shepherding his father Jacob's flocks (Genesis 37)
- Moses spent years taking care of the flocks of his father-in-law Jethro (Exodus 3)

Coincidentally, it was when Moses was out watching over those sheep that a Voice called to him from a burning bush to go to Pharaoh and demand that God's people be set free. More than any other figure in the Hebrew Bible, however, David makes the connection between shepherds and God. In numerous places, most notably in the book of Psalms, God's own character is tied to shepherding:

> The Lord is my shepherd, I shall not want. He makes me lie down in green pastures; he leads me beside still waters; he restores my soul. He leads me in right paths for his name's sake. Even though I walk through the darkest valley, I fear no evil; for you are with me; your rod and your staff—they comfort me. —Psalm 23:1–4

> The Lord is the strength of his people; he is the saving refuge of his anointed. O save your people, and bless your heritage; be their shepherd, and carry them forever.
> —Psalm 28:8–9

> Give ear, O Shepherd of Israel, you who lead Joseph like a flock! —Psalm 80:1

Jacob, summarizing his life as he lay on his deathbed, declared that God had been his "*shepherd all of his life to this day*" (Genesis 48:24).

> "He will feed his flock like a shepherd; he will gather the lambs in his arms, and carry them in his bosom, and gently lead the mother sheep." —Isaiah 40:11
> "So I will attend to you for your evil doings, says the Lord. Then I myself will gather the

remnant of my flock out of all the lands
where I have driven them, and I will bring
them back to their fold, and they shall be
fruitful and multiply." —Jeremiah 23:2–3

"For thus says the Lord God: I myself will
search for my sheep, and will seek them out.
As shepherds seek out their flocks when
they are among their scattered sheep, so I
will seek out my sheep. I will rescue them
from all the places to which they have been
scattered on a day of clouds and thick
darkness.... I myself will be the shepherd of
my sheep, and I will make them lie down,
says the Lord God." —Ezekiel 34:11–12, 15

The Hebrews weren't the only ones in the ancient
world to make this connection. King Hammurabi of
Babylon called himself a shepherd, and centuries
later Homer regularly styled the Greek chiefs as
shepherds of their people.

But try telling any of that to the official prophets
in the court of Jeroboam II, ruler of the northern
Kingdom of Israel from 786 to 746 BCE. They didn't
want Amos near the holy shrines or for that matter
anywhere in the kingdom.

They told this "mere shepherd" to shut up and go
back home to the southern Kingdom of Judah where
he belonged:

"O seer, go, flee away to the land of Judah,
earn your bread there, and prophesy there;

but never again prophesy at Bethel, for it is
the king's sanctuary, and it is a temple of
the kingdom." —Amos 7:12–13

Yet Amos humbly and forcefully stood his
ground: "I am no prophet, nor a prophet's son; but I
am a herdsman, and dresser of sycamore trees, and
the Lord took me from following the flock, and the
Lord said to me, 'Go, prophesy to my people Israel.'
Now therefore hear the word of the Lord" (7:14–15).

King Jeroboam II is widely regarded as one of the
brighter lights in the long, dismal string of leaders
who followed the reign of King Solomon. His once-
impressive empire soon was divided in two, Israel to
the north and Judah to the south. Under Jeroboam's rule a few generations later, Israel reached its
greatest prosperity and power.

> *"I am no prophet, nor a prophet's
> son; but I am a herdsman, and
> dresser of sycamore trees, and
> the Lord took me from following
> the flock, and the Lord said to me,
> 'Go, prophesy to my people
> Israel.' Now therefore hear the
> word of the Lord."*
> **—Amos 7:14–15**

Jeroboam and his kingdom were more than a bit
lucky, though. During this time Israel expanded

northward, thanks to the weakness of the city-states of Hamath and Damascus and southward at the expense of Judah. More importantly, the great powers of the time were anything but great: Assyria was weakened and preoccupied with internal matters and military excursions elsewhere. Syria had seen better days and was in decline. And so Jeroboam took advantage of all that by extending his reach militarily, encouraging trade, and building up his storehouse of wealth.

When Amos came from Judah to bring the "word of the Lord," he found a proud and prosperous civilization. Farmers produced bumper crops in well–maintained rural areas and elegant cities boasted exclusive neighborhoods filled with palaces not just for royalty (as was typical for the times) but the privileged and moneyed classes. All of this was undergirded by a strong standing army.

Rabbi Abraham Joshua Heschel, regarded by many as the preeminent Jewish scholar focusing on the Hebrew prophets, described the situation in Israel:

> The rich had their summer and winter palaces adorned with costly ivory (3:15), gorgeous couches with damask pillows (3:12), on which they reclined at their sumptuous feasts. They planted pleasant vineyards, anointed themselves with precious oils (6:4–6; 5:11), their women, compared by Amos to the fat cows of Bashan, were addicted to wine (4:1). At the

same time there was no justice in the land (3:10), the poor were afflicted, exploited, even sold into slavery (2:6-8; 5:11), and the judges were corrupt (5:12).[1]

Into this situation came Amos, a shepherd, with a warning:

> Woe to you who think you live on easy
>   street in Zion, who think Mount
>   Samaria is the good life.
> You assume you're at the top of the heap,
>   voted the number-one best place to live.
> Well, wake up and look around. Get off your
>   pedestal. Take a look at Calneh.
> Go and visit Great Hamath. Look in on Gath
>   of the Philistines.
> Doesn't that take you off your high horse?
>   Compared to them, you're not much are
>   you?
> Woe to you who are rushing headlong to
>   disaster! Catastrophe is just around the
>   corner!
> Woe to those who live in luxury and expect
>   everyone else to serve them!
> Woe to those who live only for today,
>   indifferent to the fate of others!
> Woe to the playboys, the playgirls, who
>   think life is a party held just for them!
> Woe to those addicted to feeling good—life
>   without pain! Those obsessed with
>   looking good—life without wrinkles!

They could not care less about their country
   going to ruin.
But here's what's *really* coming: a forced
   march into exile.
They'll leave the country whining, a rag-tag
   bunch of good-for-nothings.
                    —Amos 6:1–7 *The Message*

Ouch.

Probably the most important key to understanding what was happening in Israel at this time
is this: Amos's message highlighted obvious disparity between the haves and the have-nots. An
extremely wealthy class felt "secure on the mountain
of Samaria" (6:1) while at the same time they
"oppress[ed] the poor" and "crush[ed] the needy"
(4:1).

> **"There was no justice in the
> land , the poor were afflicted,
> exploited, even sold into
> slavery, and the judges were
> corrupt."**

Society's elites wallowed in their luxuries while
blind to everything and everybody else. Often in
such a situation, religious activity (presupposed by
moral guidelines) dwindles. But here, it was just the
opposite.

Amos tells us the traditional cultic centers of
Gilgal and Bethel were mobbed by worshipers, their

sacrificial altars filled with the blood and carcasses of animals (4:4, 5:5, 5:21–24).

We need to look closely at those worshipers' motives, however. The foundation for this constant activity at the holy shrines was the people's inadequate view of God and understanding of covenant. They viewed their economic prosperity (and, consequently, their international standing won by military victories) as divine approval and blessing.

How did the people understand their responsibilities and obligations? Apparently, it was limited to a public display of elaborate worship practices: the bigger the show, the more often it took place, the more obvious it became (at least to them) that Israel was God's favorite and was, therefore, guaranteed protection, stability, and opulence.

It's easy to picture that society's elites and rulers imagining just how impressive all this must be to other, "lesser" nations. Yet at the same time there appears to be little recognition of the people's moral responsibility to society as a whole and, especially, to those at the bottom end of the economic spectrum.

Although Amos never uses the word "covenant," the concept is implicit in his thought throughout the book that bears his name:

"I brought you up out of the land of Egypt,
and led you forty years in the wilderness, to
possess the land of the Amorite. And I
raised up some of your children to be

prophets and some of your youths to be nazirites. Is it not indeed so, O people of Israel? says the Lord." —2:10–11

"You only have I known of all the families of the earth; therefore I will punish you for all your iniquities." —3:2

"The end has come upon *my people* Israel...." —8:2

It would be a mistake to conclude that Israel's "problem" was prosperity. No, the problem was in how they viewed this material abundance: as proof of God's blessing and exclusive protection. To further compound matters, they believed the only response necessary was lavish worship. That's why the shrines (their alternative to the Jerusalem Temple) were constantly busy with practically nonstop sacrifices.

Moral responsibility for their fellow countrymen, much less foreigners, may not have even occurred to them. Amos was characteristically blunt:

"Come to Bethel—and transgress; to Gilgal—and multiply transgression; bring your sacrifices every morning, your tithes every three days; bring a thank offering of leavened bread, and proclaim freewill offerings, publish them; for so you love to do, O people of Israel! says the Lord God. I gave you cleanness of teeth in all your cities,

and lack of bread in all your places, yet you
did not return to me, says the Lord."
—4:4–6

"I hate, I despise your festivals, and I take
no delight in your solemn assemblies. Even
though you offer me your burnt offerings
and grain offerings, I will not accept them;
and the offerings of well–being of your
fatted animals I will not look upon. Take
away from me the noise of your songs; I will
not listen to the melody of your harps. But
let justice roll down like waters, and
righteousness like an ever-flowing stream."
—5:21–24

No doubt Amos was familiar with the long
tradition within Israel of how the attitude of
worshipers validates worship: "Who shall ascend
the hill of the Lord? And who shall stand in his holy
place? Those who have clean hands and pure hearts,
who do not lift up their souls to what is false, and do
not swear deceitfully. They will receive blessing
from the Lord, and vindication from the God of their
salvation" (Psalm 24:3–5).

The words "justice" and "righteousness" are
central to Amos's prophetic message. While they are
closely related, it's important to understand the
difference, particularly within Hebrew thought and
tradition.

The image of a blindfolded Lady Justice, who
balances scales in one hand and a sword in the other

(signifying objectivity and fairness) is commonplace in 21st-century, Western culture. It has its roots in ancient Egypt, if not farther back, and blossomed in Greek and Roman culture. The operation of an impartial legal system based on morality, equality, and fairness is a given today. The ancient Hebrews approached this subject in a different manner.

Let's begin with two Hebrew words:

• *Mishpat:* the judgment given by a judge and, as such, this word can mean justice, ordinance, norm, legal right, or law; it signifies a mode of action.

• *Tsedakah* [pronounced "said-ah-caw"]: may be rendered as "righteousness"; it is a quality of a person or nation and goes beyond justice (which is exact or strict) and implies kindness, generosity, and benevolence; it is associated with a burning compassion for the oppressed; it is significant that especially in later Hebrew thinking *tsedakah* is associated with *hesed* (mercy, loving-kindness, steadfast love)

> "Teach me to do your will, for you are my God. Let your good spirit lead me on a level path. For your name's sake, O Lord, preserve my life. In your righteousness bring me out of trouble. In your steadfast love cut off my enemies, and destroy all my adversaries, for I am your servant."
> —Psalm 143:10–12

"Thus says the Lord: Do not let the wise boast in their wisdom, do not let the mighty boast in their might, do not let the wealthy boast in their wealth; but let those who boast, boast in this, that they understand and know me, that I am the Lord; I act with steadfast love, justice, and righteousness in the earth, for in these things I delight, says the Lord." —Jeremiah 9:23–24

Prophets within the long history of Israel (and Amos certainly is characteristic) were far more concerned with the absence of righteousness rather than the absence of laws. Rather than sharing in a concern for the equal administration of laws (as in the Greco-Roman tradition), prophets were highly motivated by the presence of *injustice*.

> ### *"Prophets within Israel were far more concerned with the absence of righteousness rather than the absence of laws."*

They cared not only about the acts of scoundrels but those of prominent, highly respected pillars of society. Certainly the prophets considered justice a good thing, perhaps even a supreme ideal. But they pointed out how society lacked a sense of the monstrosity of *injustice*.

A unique contribution of the prophets was their "remorseless unveiling of injustice and oppression, in their comprehension of social, political, and religious evils. They were not concerned with the definition, but with the predicament, of justice, with the fact that those called upon to apply it defied it."[2]

Furthermore, Rabbi Heschel adds this about the prophetic calling:

> Prophecy is not a private affair. The prophet isn't concerned with his personal salvation, and the background of his experiences is the life of the people. The aim is not personal illumination, but the illumination of a people; not a spiritual self-enhancement, but a mission to lead the people to the service of God. The prophet is nothing without his people.[3]

Prophets, then, were advocates and champions, speaking on behalf of those in society who were too weak to plead their own cause. They interfered, accusing the so-called "good folks in society" of multiple wrongs inflicted on other people. They stuck their noses in other peoples' business and, therefore, were often criticized for being irresponsible and imprudent.

Yet a true prophet simply would not, or perhaps could not, tolerate wrongs done to others. As a result, they called on people to be champions of the poor:

"Wash yourselves; make yourselves clean;
remove the evil of your doings from before
my eyes; cease to do evil, learn to do good;
seek justice, rescue the oppressed, defend
the orphan, plead for the widow."
—Isaiah 1:16–17

What the Lord requires is far more than doing
one's duty. To love (in the sense of *hesed*) implies an
almost insatiable thirst, a passionate craving. It
means to move the core of one's inner life from a
concern for the self (ego) to a concern for others,
especially the oppressed, disadvantaged, and
marginalized.

"O God, you are my God, I seek you, my
soul thirsts for you; my flesh faints for you,
as in a dry and weary land where there is no
water. So I have looked upon you in the
sanctuary, beholding your power and glory.
Because your steadfast love is better than
life, my lips will praise you. So I will bless
you as long as I live; I will lift up my hands
and call on your name. My soul is satisfied
as with a rich feast, and my mouth praises
you with joyful lips when I think of you on
my bed, and meditate on you in the watches
of the night; for you have been my help, and
in the shadow of your wings I sing for joy.
My soul clings to you; your right hand
upholds me." —Psalm 63:1–8

"Seek good and not evil, that you may live;
and so the Lord, the God of hosts, will be
with you, just as you have said. Hate evil
and love good, and establish justice in the
gate; it may be that the Lord, the God of
hosts, will be gracious to the remnant of
Joseph." —Amos 5:14–16

"'With what shall I come before the Lord,
and bow myself before God on high? Shall I
come before him with burnt offerings, with
calves a year old? Will the Lord be pleased
with thousands of rams, with ten thousands
of rivers of oil? Shall I give my firstborn for
my transgression, the fruit of my body for
the sin of my soul?' He has told you, O
mortal, what is good; and what does the
Lord require of you but to do justice, and to
love kindness, and to walk humbly with
your God?" —Micah 6:6–8

"Zion shall be redeemed by justice, and
those in her who repent, by righteousness."
—Isaiah 1:27

Divine love (*hesed*) is central to one of Jesus'
most memorable parables: the lost sheep. Versions
of this parable appear in Matthew 18 and Luke 15:

Now all the tax collectors and sinners were
coming near to listen to him. And the
Pharisees and the scribes were grumbling

and saying, "This fellow welcomes sinners
and eats with them." So he told them this
parable: "Which one of you, having a
hundred sheep and losing one of them, does
not leave the ninety-nine in the wilderness
and go after the one that is lost until he
finds it? When he has found it, he lays it on
his shoulders and rejoices. And when he
comes home, he calls together his friends
and neighbors, saying to them, 'Rejoice with
me, for I have found my sheep that was
lost.' Just so, I tell you, there will be more
joy in heaven over one sinner who repents
than over ninety-nine righteous persons
who need no repentance." —Luke 15:1–7

Typically, this parable is understood as showing
God's love for each and every individual in the world
and, as a result, God's desire to offer eternal salvation to them. Our responsibility, as Jesus' disciples,
is to share the good news of God's saving power as
widely as possible so that every individual has
opportunity to accept.

There are additional ways to understand this
parable. Two basic roles for Jesus can be combined
here: *prophet* and *Good Shepherd*. As shown already, the Hebrew prophets core concern was with
others rather than with themselves.

Prophets are relentless in pointing out injustice
and being advocates and champions for the disadvantaged, marginalized, and victimized in society.
In doing so they assume the necessity and rightness

of a just society, but they go beyond that to recognize that not everyone shares in the benefits of the "sheepfold."

> ### *"What is true of individual prophets is expanded and multiplied among faith communities that understand themselves to be prophetic people."*

Prophets of God, then, can be understood within the broad umbrella of "God's shepherding activity." They will not give up until each and every victim of injustice is identified and included within society's care. They, too, have every right to share in God's abundance and blessings.

Prophets take it a step even further, to point out the systemic causes of injustice, challenging the "powers that be" to repent and return to God's "sheepfold."

What is true of individual prophets is expanded and multiplied among faith communities that understand themselves to be prophetic people. Together they are called to be champions and advocates, to stand with the poor and oppressed. They will confront societies that function in ways contrary to God's ways. They will not rest until injustice is eliminated.

Notes
1. Abraham J. Heschel, *The Prophets* (New York: Harper & Row, 1st ed., 1962; Perennial Classics ed., 2001), p. 33
2. Ibid., 260.
3. Ibid., 462.

For Reflection & Discussion

1. How have shepherds played recurring roles throughout the Bible? Why do you suppose that is?
2. In your own words, describe the situation in the northern kingdom of Israel at the time of Amos's prophetic ministry? What was the core of his message? How was it received by both the powerful and the people in general?
3. Why did Amos have such a problem with the constant activity at the shrines of Bethel and Gilgal? How did that relate to the idea of moral responsibility for both Israelites and foreigners?
4. Respond to the quoted statement by Abraham J. Heschel that the prophets' "aim is not personal illumination, but the illumination of a people; not a spiritual self-enhancement, but a mission to lead the people to the service of God. The prophet is nothing without his people."
5. Why were the Hebrew prophets such as Amos so concerned with injustice, as compared to the Greco-Roman focus on equal administration of laws? How did this compel them to become advocates and champions of those in society too weak to plead their own cause?
6. Discuss Jesus' parable of the lost sheep (as found in Matthew 18 and Luke 15) in light of the life and ministry of Amos, himself a former shepherd.
7. How does a prophetic community fit within the broad umbrella of God's shepherding activity?

Chapter 4

Hosea: Whoring after Idols

Start reading the Book of Hosea and in no time at all it becomes clear this is one of the strangest stories in all of the Hebrew Bible, which, of course, is saying something! Hosea, a prophet in the northern Kingdom of Israel not too long after the time of Amos, gets instructions from God:

- He is told to marry a woman named Gomer, the daughter of Diblaim. The text describes her in various places as a whore, a harlot, or a prostitute. Yet it's somewhat unclear whether those terms describe her *before* the marriage or just at some point later on. (At least one Jewish scholar contends the Hebrew word translated as "harlot" is more accurately a woman "disposed to *become* a harlot, a woman filled with the spirit of whoredom.")

- Hosea and Gomer have three children (two boys and a girl). God tells him to give them symbolic names: *Jezreel* (an often-bloody place where Queen Jezebel jumped to her death from a palace window—her body then devoured by wild dogs—

73

and where King Jehu, who followed Ahab on
Israel's throne, murdered Ahab's 70 sons); *Lo-
ruhamah* ("Not Pitied"); and *Lo-ammi* ("Not My
People"). The first name was a token of the coming
destruction of the dynasty of Jehu; the final two
were signs of God's threatened rejection of Israel.

• After a few years Gomer commits adultery,
although it could be that she either returns to
prostitution or is drawn to it for the first time.
There is some indication that she's involved in the
Baal fertility cult as a sacred prostitute. The name
Baal actually means "husband." Human sexual acts
were an important part of the Baal cult to ensure
bountiful harvests and fertile livestock. Eventually
God instructs Hosea to forgive her and resume the
marriage.

• At the beginning of chapter 3, the Lord once more
gives instruction to Hosea: "Go, love a woman who
has a lover and is an adulteress, just as the Lord
loves the people of Israel, though they turn to
other gods and love raisin cakes" (a food perhaps
associated with the Baal cult). It's unclear whether
this woman is Gomer or perhaps a second wife for
Hosea. In any event, Hosea buys her from her
lover (or perhaps out of prostitution) for 15 shekels
of silver, a homer of barley, and a measure of wine.
Although she becomes part of Hosea's household
as his "wife," she is forbidden to have sexual
intercourse with any man, including Hosea.

• All this is a direct reflection of the symbolic hus-
band/wife relationship God has with Israel and a
theological commentary on the lengthy, frequently
broken history of Israel's covenant with God.

Both Jewish and Christian biblical scholars have been trying to understand and explain all this for a long, long time. There is no consensus, but it's worth some of our time to attempt to unpack the details and discern what, if anything, it might mean for us Christians today.

"A woman who committed adultery could not remain a man's wife. He was required to expel her from the household."

The Israelite legal code was clear about how Hosea *should* deal with Gomer. A woman who committed adultery could not remain a man's wife. He was required to expel her from the household, for he was not allowed to live with her. Furthermore, there would be no pity for the children. They would be known as "children of harlotry," because the one who had conceived them had acted shamefully.

But Hosea was not just another Hebrew male; he was a prophet! Considering the entire narrative as a whole, it's clear that God's way (involving forgiveness and redemption) is higher than the legal way.

Still, many commentators through the centuries have found it morally repugnant for God to command a prophet to marry—and subsequently to remarry—an adulterous woman. One way around that is to suggest that maybe this whole incident was either a vision/dream or that the story was told as a parable or allegory.

The first problem with these approaches is that whatever is morally repugnant in real life is no more defensible if it's presented as a vision or an allegory.

Besides, Hosea gives no indication it's anything other than what it literally appears to be.

If it were an allegory then *all* the parts would have symbolic meanings, and that is not the case with Gomer's name. Neither is there any symbolic significance in that there are two boys and one girl born to Hosea and Gomer (it was common practice for prophets to give symbolic names to real children, however).

Finally, why would Hosea go to such lengths to tell such an incredible, fictitious story about his wife and children? By holding them up to ridicule he did the same for himself and, perhaps, even the character of God who was behind it all.

Other commentators have suggested that this was all a dramatic, public demonstration of God's actual rejection of the people of Israel. However, Hosea never proclaimed—*only threatened*—rejection. It doesn't appear to be in keeping with Hosea's sensitive nature that he should spend years of his life contracting a marriage, having children, dealing with an adulterous wife, and experiencing considerable sorrow just so the public could learn a lesson about God.

As difficult as it might be for us 21st-century Christians who are so used to reading much of the Old Testament as metaphor, parable, allegory, simile, or other figures of speech, **what we have here in the first three chapters of Hosea just may be an actual example of literal truth!**

The events of Hosea's life affected him deeply and personally regardless of their effect on the general public. In time he no doubt became aware that his own experience was something of a reflection of God's sorrow for Israel. As Abraham J. Heschel explained:

The marriage of Hosea was no symbolic representation of real facts, no act of re-creating or repeating events in the history of Israel or experiences in the inner life of God. Its meaning was not objective, inherent in the marriage, but subjective, evocative. Only by living through in his own life what the divine Consort of Israel experienced, was the prophet able to attain sympathy for the divine situation. The marriage was a lesson, an illustration, rather than a symbol or a sacrament. Its purpose was not to demonstrate divine attitudes to the people, but to educate Hosea himself in the understanding of divine sensibility.[1]

Rabbi Heschel concludes that this changed everything for Hosea:

The tragic disturbance in the relationship between God and Israel must have deter-mined decisively his attitude and outlook. Hosea, who again and again emphasized the unchanging devotion of God to Israel, was not simply an advocate of the people. His mind was powerfully affected by the embit-terment of God, echoed in his own sympa-thetic experience.[2]

Hosea's prophetic ministry was complex. He stood between God and Israel as both responsive to the divine will and responsible for the future of his people. We can probably never fully understand the tensions involved.

In much the same way, we can only begin to imagine the turmoil and torment of his personal and family life.

Looking back over many centuries, we are at least fortunate to discover this prophet whose language skills help us glimpse a measure of his character and mission.

Hosea shared characteristics of prophetic speech and action with his predecessor Amos. Amos preferred to utter "Thus says the Lord" while Hosea relied on the first-person pronoun to let his hearers know the words were God's. Throughout the book that bears his name, Hosea uses the divine name "Yahweh" (translated as "the Lord" in the RSV and NRSV, among others) rather than the more general name for God, "Elohim." The first name comes from the Hebrew verb form for "I Am," which ties it directly to Moses' experience at the burning bush and on Mount Sinai (Horeb).

> *Amos preferred to utter "Thus says the Lord" while Hosea relied on the first-person pronoun to let his hearers know the words were God's.*

Hosea was a master in using word pictures to get his hearer's attention. His metaphors and similies portrayed the nature of Yahweh and the condition of Israel before its God. They were drawn from all areas of daily life to convey his message.

Yahweh is like a husband (2:2), a father (11:1), a physician (7:1) a fowler (7:12), a lion (5:14) a leopard (13:7), a she-bear (13:8), the dew (14:5), the dawn

(6:3), the rain (6:3), a cypress (14:8) a moth (5:12), and dry rot (5:12).

Israel is like a wife (2:2), a sick person (5:13), a silly dove (7:11), a trained heifer (10:11), a luxuriant grapevine (10:1), grapes (9:10), the early fig (9:10), a lily (14:5), an olive tree (14:6) a woman in labor (13:13), an unborn son (13:13) an oven (7:4), a cake of bread (7:8) a bow (7:16), morning mist and dew (13:3), chaff blown from the threshing floor (13:3), and smoke that rises from a window (13:3).

Like other Hebrew prophets Hosea emphasized several words and phrases throughout his writings:

- **Hesed:** steadfast love, kindness (used particularly in regard to God's attitude toward Israel)
- **Tsedakah:** righteousness
- **Emunah** and **emeth:** faithfulness
- **Rachamin:** mercy, compassion (especially for those in need)
- **Mishpat:** justice
- **Da'ath elohim:** knowledge of God

This last term holds a key to understanding the core of Hosea's prophetic ministry. His main complaint against the people of Israel is that they do not know God. The Hebrew verb generally translated as "to know" is *yada*, which can often mean "to be acquainted with." But not always.

In Hebrew as well as other Semitic languages it signifies sexual union. That's why even today in popular culture, sexual activity is sometimes jokingly referred to as "knowing someone in the biblical sense."

The Hebrew-language meaning is more extensive than that, however. Knowledge can also include inner understanding, feeling, and a deep connection with the soul. Throughout the Hebrew Bible the meaning of knowledge encompasses having sympathy, pity, or affection for someone. That then leads to an emotional and spiritual connection.

The first example of a human being's emotional attachment and inner commitment to another is recorded in Genesis 4:1: "Adam knew [*yada*] Eve his wife, and she conceived and bore Cain."

Obviously, this scripture verse refers first of all to an intimate sexual relationship, but the way it's used may well refer to an emotional as well as sexual relationship, encompassing their entire beings. A better translation might then be, "Adam *attached* himself to Eve his wife...."

Joseph, one of the 12 sons of Isaac (Israel), became second only to Pharaoh in Egypt and reordered the country's entire agricultural system. By doing so he saved the people from starvation during the coming seven years of famine.

Yet after his death we are told, "Now a new king arose over Egypt, who did not *know* Joseph" (Exodus 1:8). Even if this new king didn't know Joseph personally (which is doubtful), he most certainly must have known of him. What the writer of Exodus most likely meant here is that the new king simply didn't care for, actively disliked, or maybe even despised Joseph (who was, after all, a foreigner).

Something similar was probably the case with the sons of Eli, who was a judge over Israel and the high priest at the important sanctuary of Shiloh: "They were base men; they *knew not* the Lord" (1 Samuel 2:12 KJV).

The NRSV comes closer to the deeper meaning: "Now the sons of Eli were scoundrels; they *had no regard for* the Lord." They had no inner commitment to the Lord or the religious rituals performed by the priests. "Thus the sin of the young men was very great in the sight of the Lord; for they treated the offerings of the Lord with contempt" (2:17). There was no emotional attachment for those young men, simply an opportunity to display their selfish appetites.

> *"Throughout the Hebrew Bible the meaning of knowledge encompasses having sympathy, pity, or affection for someone. That then leads to an emotional and spiritual connection."*

When the Hebrew tribes were enslaved in Egypt, "their cry under bondage came up to God. And God heard their groaning, and God remembered his covenant with Abraham, with Isaac, and with Jacob. And God saw the people of Israel and God *knew* their condition" (Exodus 2:24-25). In other words, God *had pity on* them.

A little later in Exodus we find this: "Then the Lord said, I have seen the affliction of my people who are in Egypt, and have heard their cry because of their taskmasters; I *know* their sufferings" (3:7).

What the writer of Exodus means is "I *have sympathy for*, I *am affected by*, their sufferings."

In a similar vein the psalmist wrote, "I will be glad and rejoice in your love [*hesed*], for you saw my affliction and *knew* the anguish of my soul" (Psalm 31:7 NIV).

The NRSV translates the passage this way: "I will exult and rejoice in your steadfast love, because you have seen my affliction; you *have taken heed of* my adversities." Note here the connection between divine love and knowledge.

To put it another way, God has a feeling (or pity) for the psalmist. Abraham J. Heschel connects all these various expressions of "knowing" in this way:

> The relationship between God and Israel, conceived by Hosea in terms of marital love, desertion, and the hope of new betrothal, calls not only for right action, but also for a feeling for each other on the part of those involved. It implies not only legal obligations, but also inner attitudes.
>
> In the light of his own complete emotional solidarity with God, Hosea seems to have seized upon the idea of sympathy as the essential religious requirement. The words *da'ath elohim* mean *sympathy for God*, attachment of the whole person, his love as well as his knowledge; an act of involvement, attachment or commitment to God.[3]

Israel's future, as well as Hosea's, is tied directly to this understanding of knowing [*da'ath*]: "My people are destroyed for lack of knowledge; because you have rejected knowledge, I reject you from being a priest to me. And since you have forgotten the law of your God, I also will forget your children" (Hosea 4:6 NRSV).

The contrast between the prophetic messages of Amos and Hosea is seen in what they identify as Israel's primary sin:

> I hate, I despise your festivals, and I take no delight in your solemn assemblies. Even though you offer me your burnt offerings

and grain offerings, I will not accept them;
and the offerings of well-being of your
fatted animals I will not look upon. Take
away from me the noise of your songs; I will
not listen to the melody of your harps. But
let justice roll down like waters, and
righteousness like an ever-flowing stream.
                              —Amos 5:21–24

For I desire steadfast love and not sacrifice,
the knowledge of God rather than burnt
offerings.   —Hosea 6:6

Throughout the times of both prophets, the
people of Israel repeatedly strayed from the worship
of Yahweh, breaking a covenant that was reflected in
the observance of moral law and ritual sacrifice.
    Instead they were enticed by the sensuality and
sexual practices of Baal worship, a fertility cult
celebrating the regular cycles of nature and which
lacked any moral component whatsoever.
    Amos dwelt on what God *had done* for Israel (see
Amos 2:9ff), while Hosea emphasized what God *had
felt* for Israel, which he often referred to as
Ephraim:

When Israel was a child, I loved him, and
out of Egypt I called my son. The more I
called them, the more they went from me;
they kept sacrificing to the Baals, and
offering incense to idols.
    Yet it was I who taught Ephraim to walk,
I took them up in my arms; but they did not
know that I healed them. I led them with
cords of human kindness, with bands of
love. I was to them like those who lift

83

infants to their cheeks. I bent down to them
and fed them.   —Hosea 11:1–4

So strong was Hosea's conviction of Yahweh's
great love for Israel that not even the people's sin
could extinguish it. Characteristically, each major
section of Hosea's book ends with the promise of
restoration.

Ultimately, what triumphs is the image of
Yahweh as a scorned lover who continues to woo
Israel:

> My people are bent on turning away from
> me. To the Most High [*Baal?*] they call, but
> he does not raise them up at all. How can I
> give you up, Ephraim? How can I hand you
> over, O Israel? How can I make you like
> Admah? How can I treat you like Zeboiim?
> My heart recoils within me; my compassion
> grows warm and tender. I will not execute
> my fierce anger; I will not again destroy
> Ephraim; for I am God and no mortal, the
> Holy One in your midst, and I will not come
> in wrath. —Hosea 11:7–9

The person and mission of the prophet Hosea
demonstrated a deep and abiding sympathy for God.
That, in turn, was but a reflection for Yahweh's deep
and abiding love for and knowledge of Israel.

God had been there for and with the people from
the beginning, establishing a covenantal relationship that endured despite the people's sins. In their
attempts to *know* other gods, they essentially tried
to elevate their own selfish human desires as a re-
placement for their ancestral God, Yahweh.

Human beings are still doing the same thing in our own 21st century. The Creator, who knows and loves us more than we can comprehend, strives to restore a relationship, a bond, a covenant we continually attempt to sever. Modern prophetic ministry, in sympathy with God and the community, dwells in the breach.

Notes
1. Abraham J. Heschel, *The Prophets* (New York: Harper & Row, 1st ed., 1962; Perennial Classics ed., 2001), 69.
2. Ibid.
3. Ibid., 72-73.

For Reflection & Discussion

1. In your own words recount the basic plot of this Old Testament book. What makes it so strange and unique among all the books in the Bible? Why do you think both Jewish and Christian scholars have failed to reach a consensus on its purpose and meaning?
2. How appropriate is the symbolism of a husband and wife's relationship to that of God and the people of Israel? What role does forgiveness and restoration play in this relationship?
3. The biblical text reflects a basically patriarchal view of the marital relationship. What would happen to our understanding of Hosea's prophetic ministry if we attempt to remove the patriarchy? How does that patriarchal relationship continue to define the relationship between God and humankind (or Christ and the church) today?

4. What are some of the word pictures Hosea employs for God (Yahweh) and Israel? How do these multiple metaphors and similes enrich our understanding of this relationship?
5. Review the various Hebrew words defined in this chapter: *hesed, tsedakah, emunah, rachamin, mishpat,* and *da'ath elohim.* How might the last one in the list hold a key to understanding the core of Hosea's prophetic ministry?
6. Compare the different approaches found in the prophetic messages of Amos 5:21–24 and Hosea 6:6 in regard to Israel's primary sin. Why do you think these two prophets approached the same topic in opposite ways?
7. What can a modern prophetic people learn from Hosea's "deep and abiding sympathy for God"?

Chapter 5

Jeremiah: Plucking Up and Planting

Jeremiah hated his job.

A career change, though, was simply out of the question, for he was Yahweh's prophet and Judah's chief spiritual leader. Born into a priestly household in the tribe of Benjamin, Jeremiah served initially as a priest. But destiny called:

> Now the word of the Lord came to me saying, "Before I formed you in the womb I knew you, and before you were born I consecrated you; I appointed you a prophet to the nations." —Jeremiah 1:4–5

Jeremiah tried to talk Yahweh out of this calling:

> Then I said, "Ah, Lord God! Truly I do not know how to speak, for I am only a boy." But the Lord said to me, "Do not say, 'I am only a boy'; for you shall go to all to whom I send you, and you shall speak whatever I command you. Do not be afraid of them, for I am with you to deliver you, says the Lord."

> Then the Lord put out his hand and
> touched my mouth; and the Lord said to
> me, "Now I have put my words in your
> mouth. See, today I appoint you over
> nations and over kingdoms, to pluck up and
> to pull down, to destroy and to overthrow,
> to build and to plant." —1: 6–10

Jeremiah was among the greatest of all the classical Hebrew prophets, those during and after the era of David and Solomon. There is little question that the four decades during which Jeremiah lived marked the most tumultuous and tragic period in the history of the southern Kingdom of Judah. By its end, the temple lay in ruins, along with much of the rest of Jerusalem's walled city, and many of its citizens carted off to Babylonian exile.

Numerous kings ruled, died, or were deposed during those sad years. Foreign dominance shifted from the Assyrians, who years before conquered the Kingdom of Israel in the north, to the Egyptians briefly, and then to the newest superpower, Babylon.

Tiny Judah had the misfortune of being located geographically in the midst of all that. As such, its kings faced constantly shifting threats from outside the country, along with intrigues and rivalries within. Added to that was Judah's collective memory of past glory days and a persistent theological belief that Yahweh would protect them from any and all threats.

Jeremiah's prophetic messages shared much in common with contemporaries such as Habbakuk, Micah, Amos, Hosea, and Isaiah ben Amoz (sometimes referred to as "First Isaiah"). He also delivered words of warning and condemnation for rampant injustice and idolatry, for a reliance on outward forms of religion that ignored deeper moral and ethical issues. Yet what helped set Jeremiah apart was his calling to "build and plant" as well as "destroy and overthrow."

"Jeremiah was among the greatest of all the classical Hebrew prophets, those during and after the era of David and Solomon."

His life and prophetic ministry can be understood best in the context of Judah's complicated political and religious situation.

King Josiah was one of the few bright lights in the nation's long royal line after Solomon. Well, perhaps he wasn't a truly "bright light," but compared to almost all the others at least a noticeable "blip." He's credited with starting a serious religious renewal.

Many scholars believe the Book of Deuteronomy offers a record of this reformation of temple worship and a renewed focus on Mosaic Law. In the process, foreign gods and their cultic practices lost some of their grip on everyday life in Judah. Still, Jeremiah criticized the continued overreliance on temple practices and the influence of official priests.

Josiah paid sizeable financial tributes to the Assyrians but still had to worry about threats coming from the Egyptians. In the midst of his religious and political reforms at home, Josiah led his army against Pharoah Neco II, only to be killed in battle himself. But the Egyptians couldn't take permanent advantage of his death because the Babylonians were quickly replacing the Assyrians to Judah's east.

"Jeremiah criticized the continued overreliance on temple practices and the influence of official priests."

One of Josiah's younger sons initially succeeded his father on the throne but was quickly removed by Pharoah Neco's orders. He was replaced by an older brother, Jehoiakim, whom the Egyptians could more easily control.

Sadly, he wasn't anything like his father, caring nothing for religious reforms and focused primarily on making his palace bigger and more luxurious. This not only drained much of what was left in the national treasury because of annual tribute payments to the Assyrians, Egyptians, and finally Babylonians but required virtual slavery on the part of his own people. To top it all off, Jehoiakim built a reputation for ruthless bloodshed.

Eventually he stopped tribute payments to the Babylonians, thinking the Egyptians would protect him. But before King Nebuchadrezzer could send the mighty Babylonian army against Judah, Jehoiakim died and his teenage son Jehoiachim became king. The account of his brief reign in 2 Kings 24 indicates the young king didn't share his father's enthusiasm for opposing Nebuchadrezzer.

And so when the Babylonians surrounded Jerusalem in 597 BCE, the city fell with ease. Jehoiachim and many of the city's leading citizens were taken captive to Babylon.

Nebuchadrezzer installed Zedekiah (another of Josiah's sons) as king. After ruling Judah for a decade he became discontented with his overlords and invited leaders of other vassal-states to Jerusalem to form an alliance.

Nebuchadrezzar laid siege to Jerusalem, although it took a year and a half before the city fell. Zedekiah was forced to watch his sons' execution, then he was blinded and forced into exile.

In a strange twist of fate, Jeremiah, who had continually urged Judah's kings to submit to the Babylonians, was kidnapped by pro-Egyptian radicals and lived the rest of his life in Egypt.

As we look back from our 21st-century perspective, Judah's descent into destruction and exile appears obvious, foolish, and unnecessary. Other than perhaps Jeremiah himself, those involved in this story didn't or couldn't see it with such clarity.

The people were blinded, first of all, by a sense of invulnerability. They were convinced Yahweh would protect this special people and nation no matter what. Were they not offering sacrifices in the Jerusalem Temple and observing the festivals? Wasn't that what the covenant—whether tied to Abraham or Moses or David—was all about?

"Were they not offering sacrifices in the Jerusalem Temple and observing the festivals?"

Perhaps if Josiah had lived longer and had heeded the counsel of Jeremiah everything might have turned out differently. But that didn't happen.

The king, the temple priests, the ruling elites, and the general populace simply didn't understand that rituals and sacrifices were at best a starting point. They were symbolic practices that outwardly reflected an inner, deeply spiritual relationship between the Divine and humanity.

The people's failure to live up to their responsibilities in this covenant was why the prophets continually called out the nation—from the rulers on down—for injustice, idolatry, inequality, and a multitude of other moral failings.

Rabbi Abraham J. Heschel described Israel's distress as more than just a human tragedy [*note his use of "G–d" to avoid using the divine name*]:

> With Israel's distress came the affliction of G–d, His displacement, His homelessness in the land, in the world. And the prophet's prayer, "O save us," involved not only the fate of a people. It involved the fate of G-d in relation to the people. For Israel's desertion was not merely an injury to man; it was an insult to G-d. This was the voice of G-d who felt shunned, pained, and offended:
>> Have I been a wilderness to Israel,
>> Or a land of thick darkness?
>> Why then do My people say,
>> We are free,
>> We will come no more to Thee?
>> Can a maiden forget her ornaments,
>> Or a bride her attire?
>> Yet My people have forgotten Me
>> Days without number. (Jeremiah 2:31–32) [1]

Jeremiah understood the deeper meanings of covenant. He knew that God wanted more than anything else for this special people to be faithful. In doing so the people and nation would reflect the faithfulness of God to divine promises.

Like other prophets, he used symbols and figures of speech, likening God's relationship to Israel and Judah as that of a husband and a parent. In one of his most remarkable and memorable parables,

Jeremiah drew on the Genesis account of creation in which God had formed humans from clay. He went on to envisage God as a potter who forms clay into a useful and beautiful vessel:

> The word that came to Jeremiah from the Lord: "Come, go down to the potter's house, and there I will let you hear my words." So I went down to the potter's house, and there he was working at his wheel. The vessel he was making of clay was spoiled in the potter's hand, and he reworked it into another vessel, as seemed good to him.
>
> Then the word of the Lord came to me: Can I not do with you, O house of Israel, just as this potter has done? says the Lord. Just like the clay in the potter's hand, so are you in my hand, O house of Israel.
>
> At one moment I may declare concerning a nation or a kingdom, that I will pluck up and break down and destroy it, but if that nation, concerning which I have spoken, turns from its evil, I will change my mind about the disaster that I intended to bring on it.
>
> And at another moment I may declare concerning a nation or a kingdom that I will build and plant it, but if it does evil in my sight, not listening to my voice, then I will change my mind about the good that I had intended to do to it.
>
> Now, therefore, say to the people of Judah and the inhabitants of Jerusalem: Thus says the Lord: Look, I am a potter shaping evil against you and devising a plan against you. Turn now, all of you from your

> evil way, and amend your ways and your
> doings. —Jeremiah 18:1–11

The prophet wasn't just wandering around Jerusalem one day and happened to pass by a potter's workshop, which then got him thinking. No, God sent Jeremiah there deliberately to learn a powerful lesson.

The first point worth noting is that God's intentions for Judah were not fixed: God *can* and *will* change God's own mind depending on the nation's response. This will surprise many contemporary Christians today who connect unchangeableness not only to God's basic character but actions, as well. However, the Old Testament is filled with references to God changing course when things don't work out as originally intended. For starters, think of the stories of Noah, Lot, and Jonah.

The only characteristic of God that does not change is God's love for creation, particularly when it involves the special relationship God instituted with the descendants of Abraham. In fact, God changes course when love demands it.

Where does the idea that God does not—*or cannot*—change come from? Of course, the first scripture that comes to mind is Malachi 3:6: "For I the LORD do not change; therefore you, O children of Jacob, have not perished." This relates only to God's character and nature, though, not divine activity.

Many of us have fond memories of singing a number of familiar hymns, not the least of which is the classic, "Abide with Me":

> Swift to its close ebbs out life's little day;
> Earth's joys grow dim, its glories pass away;

Change and decay in all around I see:
O thou who changest not, abide with me.[2]

Hymns are an essential and deeply meaningful part of the spiritual life of Christians. Yet we need to see those texts as a reflection of biblical insight tempered by the hymn writer's own understandings, worldview, and cultural context. This is precisely why hymnals require continual scrutiny and updating.

"God changes course when love demands it."

Jeremiah offers us a description of an actual potter working at his wheel. Not every project works out as intended, and so at times he must punch it down, knead out pockets of air inside the clay, and start over. It's what we in today's world might term tough love.

In Jeremiah's context, if the people of Judah won't respond appropriately to God's intentions—by cooperating, listening, repenting, and turning from their misguided and evil ways—then God just might change God's mind. Perhaps God will move to a Plan B or C or D or who knows where it will all lead.

Part of the challenge here is with the word "plan" in regard to God. People today commonly talk about "God's Plan," either for their life or in a bigger, more all–inclusive sense. Typically, this is something set in stone, without any room for alteration. It's then a short step to an acceptance that whatever happens, it *must be* part of God's Plan and that *"everything happens for a reason."*

Yet how can that approach be reconciled with free will and human agency? This brings us back to prophets such as Jeremiah. God loves creation and Israel/Judah so much that there will always be choices to make:

> I call heaven and earth to witness against you today that I have set before you life and death, blessings and curses. Choose life so that you and your descendants may live, loving the Lord your God, obeying him, and holding fast to him, for that means life to you and length of days, so that you may live in the land that the Lord swore to give to your ancestors, to Abraham, to Isaac, and to Jacob. —Deuteronomy 30:19–20

> Now if you are unwilling to serve the Lord, choose this day whom you will serve, whether the gods your ancestors served in the region beyond the River or the gods of the Amorites in whose land you are living; but as for me and my household, we will serve the Lord. —Joshua 24:15

The people continually struggled with the choices set before them by God. As well, there was a tension within the inner life of God. In a passage that recalls Abraham's debate with God over the threatened destruction of the city of Sodom, God indicates to Jeremiah an implied desire to avoid judgment on Judah:

> Run to and fro through the streets of Jerusalem, look around and take note! Search its squares and see if you can find one person who acts justly and seeks truth— so that I may pardon Jerusalem —Jer. 5:1

96

Maybe we should simply substitute the word "intention" whenever we encounter the idea of God's "plan." This comes closer to what inspired and prophetic biblical writers had in mind. Consider, for instance, Isaiah 55:11:

> ...so shall my word be that goes out from my
> mouth; it shall not return to me empty, but
> it shall accomplish that which I purpose,
> and succeed in the thing for which I sent it.

It's a very different matter for God to form a people and for them to live in covenantal relationship with God. God *intends* but the people have agency; they have choices to make.

Those choices inevitably will require sacrifices. Now, that's not killing animals on an altar in a temple but making choices as to how they live their lives, whether they will do this or that, deciding how they will spend their time, talents, treasure, and all the other human resources they possess.

Above all else, God intends for the kingdom of God to be established on earth as it is in heaven. This will come about, Christians believe, not simply because human beings make it so but because the response of God's people matches the ministry of Jesus Christ expressed in small and large ways throughout the entire earth.

The world is *not* waiting for a church that opens its door just to talk *about* Jesus. The world *is* waiting for a people who are formed by God, a people who live out their faith in Jesus Christ in service to their fellow human beings. This brings us right back to Jeremiah's parable of God as potter. And what God's intentions are for us right here.

There is a famous line from the movie, *Field of Dreams*: "If you build it they will come." That worked for a fictitious story of a baseball diamond built in the middle of a magical cornfield in Iowa. But it doesn't work here in regard to the covenantal relationship between God and a prophetic people.

What may work better is something along the lines of **"If God forms us, we will go."** Our "going" will be an expression of our faith in Jesus Christ, who calls us into a life of service. Yes, discipleship involves sacrifice. It means being willing to give up cherished relationships and habits and practices if necessary.

This is the way of Christ, the way God intends for God's rule to be established throughout the world.

Notes

1. Abraham Joshua Heschel, *The Prophets* (New York: Harper & Row, 1962; Perennial Classics Edition, 2001), 142-143.
2. Text by Henry Francis Lyte (1793-1847).

For Reflection & Discussion

1. How did Jeremiah try to escape his "career" as a prophet of God? Why is that important to note in any discussion of his prophetic ministry?
2. Jeremiah's long life included some of the most turbulent and distressing years of Judah's existence. How did that background undergird everything he said and did? Briefly review Judah's complicated political and religious situation in the years leading up to its destruction by Babylon.
3. Why were the people of Judah so convinced they were invulnerable to defeat and destruction? Where did that idea come from?
4. Read aloud the parable of the potter found in Jeremiah 18. What are the lessons that can be learned from it?
5. Where does the idea come from that God does not—or cannot—change? How did the image and activity of God change and develop from the early to later parts of the Old Testament?
6. What's the difference between God's "plan" and "intentions"? How does the idea of agency fit in?
7. Discuss the author's statement: "The world is not waiting for a church that opens its door just to talk about Jesus. The world is waiting for a people who are formed by God, a people who live out their faith in Jesus Christ in service to their fellow human beings." How does this relate to Jeremiah's parable of the potter?

Chapter 6

Ezekiel: God Scatters and Gathers

Dawn broke quietly over the southern Pennsylvania countryside that July 4th morning. But there would be no American Independence Day celebrations that day. No brass bands. No flags waving. No picnics in parks or on church grounds. No speeches recalling brave acts by Revolutionary War patriots.

This was July 4, 1863. For three days Union and Confederate armies had battled fiercely in the countryside around Gettysburg. More than 7,000 dead bodies lay scattered in the fields. Thousands of other soldiers suffered wounds. With only basic medical care and little knowledge of how infections spread, thousands more would die in the coming weeks and months.

But there was a sense among the area's farmers and shopkeepers, as well as military commanders, that something had to be done immediately about all those dead bodies left out in the heat and humidity of a mid-summer day in southern Pennsylvania.

And so the survivors set out to organize the corpses as best they could by military unit, then bury them in shallow graves. Making this overwhelming task even more difficult was the stench of burning horseflesh from the massive pile of more than 300 horses killed during the battles.

As noble and helpful as their emergency efforts proved to be, local residents discovered within a few weeks that rainstorms and scavenging wildlife caused body parts to once more appear above ground.

Eventually, federal government officials approved a plan to establish a military cemetery for the Union soldiers. Exhuming bodies and reburying them began that fall. Bodies of Confederate soldiers, however, were dug up and transported to various sites in Southern states, mostly in nearby Virginia.

In November, U.S. President Abraham Lincoln came to the dedication, an event memorialized by his now-famous Gettysburg Address.

By 21st-century standards, this appears primitive. But it was far removed from what usually happened after most battles in ancient times.

Typically, victorious armies thousands of years ago simply left the bodies of defeated foes in the fields to rot and stink. Wild animals and birds picked apart the festering skin, muscle, and tissue. The bones that were left, bleached dry and white in the sun.

Women and children of the dead and defeated soldiers, meanwhile, would either be killed or taken as slaves, paraded as trophies or later sacrificed to the victors' gods.

This unpleasantness brings us to a remarkable vision given to the Hebrew prophet Ezekiel late in his life. Decades before as a teenager, he had been among the first group of captives in Jerusalem to be sent into Babylonian exile from their native Judah.

A few years after that, the Babylonian army returned to demolish the city's gleaming temple, raze most of the rest of the buildings in Judah's capital city, and send even more captives to far-off Babylon.

"Typically, victorious armies thousands of years ago simply left the bodies of defeated foes in the fields to rot and stink."

A mixture of theological, social, political, and military issues combined to eliminate whatever hope might still remain among those Hebrew captives. All that serves as background for chapter 37 in the biblical book that bears Ezekiel's name:

> The hand of the LORD came upon me, and he brought me out by the spirit of the LORD and set me down in the middle of a valley; it was full of bones.
>
> He led me all around them; there were very many lying in the valley, and they were very dry. He said to me, "Mortal, can these bones live?"
>
> I answered, "O Lord GOD, you know."
>
> Then he said to me, "Prophesy to these bones, and say to them: O dry bones, hear the word of the LORD. Thus says the Lord GOD to these bones: I will cause breath to enter you, and you shall live. I will lay sinews on you, and will cause flesh to come upon you, and cover you with skin, and put breath in you, and you shall live; and you shall know that I am the LORD."
>
> So I prophesied as I had been commanded; and as I prophesied, suddenly there was a noise, a rattling, and the bones came

together, bone to its bone. I looked, and
there were sinews on them, and flesh had
come upon them, and skin had covered
them; but there was no breath in them.

Then he said to me, "Prophesy to the
breath, prophesy, mortal, and say to the
breath: Thus says the Lord GOD: Come from
the four winds, O breath, and breathe upon
these slain, that they may live."

I prophesied as he commanded me, and
the breath came into them, and they lived,
and stood on their feet, a vast multitude.
—Ezekiel 37:1–10

Imagine this remarkable vision as a "reverse
battle." It begins with dry, bleached bones to which
sinew and flesh are added. Here the bones come
together with a great rattling noise. Eventually the
prophet sees a multitude of figures that appear to be
human. Yet they aren't breathing, living creatures.

In the vision God next tells Ezekiel to speak to the
wind, which comes from all directions. In Hebrew,
the same word (*ruah*) is used for wind, breath, and
spirit. It's also the same Hebrew word used in the
opening chapters of Genesis in which God forms the
first humans from the elements of the ground before
breathing life into them.

Ezekiel, not surprisingly, is baffled. Fortunately,
the meaning of this amazing vision is made clear to
the prophet:

Then he said to me, "Mortal, these bones
are the whole house of Israel. They say, 'Our
bones are dried up, and our hope is lost; we
are cut off completely.' Therefore prophesy,
and say to them, Thus says the Lord GOD: I
am going to open your graves, and bring

you up from your graves, O my people; and
I will bring you back to the land of Israel.
And you shall know that I am the LORD,
when I open your graves, and bring you up
from your graves, O my people. I will put my
spirit within you, and you shall live, and I
will place you on your own soil; then you
shall know that I, the LORD, have spoken
and will act, says the LORD."
                              —Ezekiel 37:11–14

Perhaps this strange vision confirmed to some of
his fellow exiles that the prophet had, in fact, lost
his mind: *"Crazy old Zeke is at it again!"*

Today, we might describe it as an hallucination.
Maybe we'd more politely use mental-illness de-
scriptors such as psychosis or schizophrenia. A case
could be made that the prophet exhibited bipolar
(manic-depressive) tendencies.

Certainly, a literal rendering of this vision of
rattling skeletons coming back to life would seem
more appropriate to campfire ghost stories or scary
Halloween imagery. But that's why this should *not*
be taken literally. It should, however, be taken
seriously.

"In Hebrew, the same word (ruah) is used for wind, breath, and spirit."

From beginning to end, the book of Ezekiel is
filled with strange imagery. From boyhood, Ezekiel
had been groomed to be a temple priest in Jerusalem. That changed at age 14 when he was included
in the first wave of exiles sent to Babylon (sometimes referred to as Chaldea).

105

Several years later he had his first visionary experience in which he was called to become a prophet: a fiery chariot driven by four human-like creatures, whose faces gave the appearance of a lion, an ox, and an eagle as well as a human. There was fire, lightning, wheels spinning inside other wheels, enormous wings, a massive dome capped by a sapphire throne, and a splendid rainbow.

> This was the appearance of the likeness of the glory of the Lord. When I saw it, I fell on my face, and I heard the voice of someone speaking. He said to me: O mortal, stand up on your feet, and I will speak with you. And when he spoke to me, a spirit entered into me and set me on my feet; and I heard him speaking to me. He said to me, Mortal, I am sending you to the people of Israel, to a nation of rebels who have rebelled against me; they and their ancestors have transgressed against me to this very day.
> The descendants are impudent and stubborn. I am sending you to them, and you shall say to them, "Thus says the Lord GOD." Whether they hear or refuse to hear (for they are a rebellious house), they shall know that there has been a prophet among them. And you, O mortal, do not be afraid of them, and do not be afraid of their words, though briers and thorns surround you and you live among scorpions; do not be afraid of their words, and do not be dismayed at their looks, for they are a rebellious house.
> You shall speak my words to them, whether they hear or refuse to hear; for they are a rebellious house. —Ezekiel 1:28–2:7

"Whether they hear or refuse to hear ... they shall know that there has been a prophet among them."

An important consideration for Ezekiel's prophetic ministry is the gap between the first and final deportations of Jews from their homeland in Judah to Babylon. These deportations are dated to 597 BCE for the first, with others dated at 587/586 BCE, and 582/581 BCE respectively. Keep in mind that Ezekiel was taken in the first wave of deportations.

There is some reason to believe many Jerusalem Jews ridiculed their exiled brethren in Babylon. Not only did they offer little comfort to the exiles but may have gone so far as to claim Jerusalem was now a much better place because those in exile were no longer there. Jeremiah, for his part, criticized this idea with his vision of the baskets of figs:

> The LORD showed me two baskets of figs placed before the temple of the LORD. This was after King Nebuchadrezzar of Babylon had taken into exile from Jerusalem King Jeconiah son of Jehoiakim of Judah, together with the officials of Judah, the artisans, and the smiths, and had brought them to Babylon.
>
> One basket had very good figs, like first-ripe figs, but the other basket had very bad figs, so bad that they could not be eaten.
>
> And the LORD said to me, "What do you see, Jeremiah?" I said, "Figs, the good figs very good, and the bad figs very bad, so bad that they cannot be eaten."

Then the word of the Lord came to me:
Thus says the Lord, the God of Israel: Like
these good figs, so I will regard as good the
exiles from Judah, whom I have sent away
from this place to the land of the Chaldeans.
I will set my eyes upon them for good,
and I will bring them back to this land. I will
build them up, and not tear them down; I
will plant them, and not pluck them up. I
will give them a heart to know that I am the
Lord; and they shall be my people and I will
be their God, for they shall return to me
with their whole heart.
But thus says the Lord: Like the bad figs
that are so bad they cannot be eaten, so will
I treat King Zedekiah of Judah, his officials,
the remnant of Jerusalem who remain in
this land, and those who live in the land of
Egypt. I will make them a horror, an evil
thing, to all the kingdoms of the earth—a
disgrace, a byword, a taunt, and a curse in
all the places where I shall drive them.
And I will send sword, famine, and
pestilence upon them, until they are utterly
destroyed from the land that I gave to them
and their ancestors. —Jeremiah 24:1–10

Ezekiel's calling initially was to be God's watchman among the exiles who believed God had abandoned them in Babylon. Eventually they would be
joined by more exiles. All of them still suffered from
a narrow view of their national relationship with
God.

Ezekiel's remarkable view of God, however, was
not limited by the land of Israel, the Jerusalem
Temple, or the daily presence and reminder of the
Babylonian gods.

He received divine direction that he should not fear his audience or base success on the people's response. Instead, he should focus on speaking God's words.

This was somewhat similar to Jeremiah's prophetic calling. He tried unsuccessfully to persuade God that he was just too young to accept such a calling. God's response:

> "Do not say, 'I am only a boy'; for you shall go to all to whom I send you, and you shall speak whatever I command you. Do not be afraid of them, for I am with you to deliver you, says the Lord." —Jeremiah 1:7–8

Perhaps as an added effect if not a burden, God made it impossible for Ezekiel to speak on his own. He could not vocalize his own thoughts, just those God commanded him to utter:

> The spirit entered into me, and set me on my feet; and he spoke with me and said to me: Go, shut yourself inside your house. As for you, mortal, cords shall be placed on you, and you shall be bound with them, so that you cannot go out among the people; and I will make your tongue cling to the roof of your mouth, so that you shall be speechless and unable to reprove them; for they are a rebellious house.
> But when I speak with you, I will open your mouth, and you shall say to them, "Thus says the Lord GOD"; let those who will hear, hear; and let those who refuse to hear, refuse; for they are a rebellious house.
> —Ezekiel 3:24–27

The most popular explanation among the Jewish exiles for their situation was that their parents had sinned but they were the ones to suffer the consequences. God hadn't treated their generation justly, they reasoned. Ezekiel took a different approach. Each person carried responsibility for his or her own, individual actions:

> The word of the Lord came to me: What do you mean by repeating this proverb concerning the land of Israel, "The parents have eaten sour grapes, and the children's teeth are set on edge"?
> As I live, says the Lord God, this proverb shall no more be used by you in Israel. Know that all lives are mine; the life of the parent as well as the life of the child is mine: it is only the person who sins that shall die."
> —Ezekiel 18:1–4

Why, then, had God apparently executed judgment against all of Judah? The prophet offered a three-fold answer.

First, the so-called prophets in Judah had deceived the people by continually reassuring them of divine protection and safety when, in fact, the opposite was the truth. They had cried "Peace, when there was no peace."

Second, the priests did not teach the people how to be holy. Instead, they encouraged only an outward expression of ritual piety. The people proudly went to the temple and made a show of their offerings and sacrifices.

Third, the nation's leaders, who should have been acting as "shepherds on behalf of God," failed to establish justice in the land. As a result, most people were oppressed and had nobody to intercede to God on their behalf for mercy.

Once Jerusalem had fallen and the temple destroyed, Ezekiel's role transitioned from watchman or sentry to that of bearer of hope. The prophet thus began to prepare the people for their eventual return to their ancestral homeland. Before that to happen, the people would need to be transformed and reinvigorated. Above all, they would need to recognize that their future was completely dependent on the direct action of God:

> Thus says the Lord GOD: On the day that I cleanse you from all your iniquities, I will cause the towns to be inhabited, and the waste places shall be rebuilt. The land that was desolate shall be tilled, instead of being the desolation that it was in the sight of all who passed by.
>
> And they will say, "This land that was desolate has become like the garden of Eden; and the waste and desolate and ruined towns are now inhabited and fortified."
>
> Then the nations that are left all around you shall know that I, the LORD, have rebuilt the ruined places, and replanted that which was desolate; I, the LORD, have spoken, and I will do it.
>
> Thus says the Lord GOD: I will also let the house of Israel ask me to do this for them: to increase their population like a flock. Like the flock for sacrifices, like the flock at Jerusalem during her appointed festivals, so shall the ruined towns be filled with flocks of people. Then they shall know that I am the LORD. —Ezekiel 36:33–38

This brings us back to the vision of the dry bones. While human beings can destroy life, whether on a battlefield or any number of other ways, only God can create or renew life. The example of the prophet Ezekiel shows clearly that what counts in the end is that people must acknowledge God's claim on their life and seek to glorify God's holy name.

This is no one-way street. There must be a back-and-forth aspect to the relationship between human beings and God. This was true for Ezekiel, as it was for all the ancient prophets.

Rabbi Abraham J. Heschel put it this way:

> The prophetic personality, far from being dissolved, is intensely present and fervently involved in what he perceives. The prophetic act is an encounter of a concrete person and the living God. The prophet is responsive, not only receptive.
>
> The act is often a dialogue in which consciousness of time, remembrance of events of the past, and concern with the plight of the present come into play. God as a person confronts the prophet as a person: God in His pathos, and the prophet in history with an awareness of a personal mission to a particular people.[1]

Rabbi Heschel goes on to explain that in "his visions the prophet's personal identity does not melt away, but, on the contrary, gains power under the overwhelming impact of the event. Even if the event takes him by storm, his consciousness remains undisturbed, free to observe and free to respond."[2]

Exile can be expressed in many ways, not just with physical distance. For 21st-century prophetic people, it may arise in social, political, economic, or spiritual ways.

What people enduring exile most often experience, perhaps, is a sense of hopelessness. For whatever they had in the past has been taken away, and they are unsure if life will, or can, ever return to normal.

For Christians, the concept of hope is tied to Jesus Christ and the promise of resurrection and restoration. This is not limited to some far-off, heavenly goal but finds expression here in this world.

How many millions of people throughout the world are suffering their own exilic experience, waiting to hear a word of hope? That is precisely where a prophetic people are called to be.

Notes

1. Abraham Joshua Heschel, *The Prophets* (New York: Harper & Row, 1962; Perennial Classics Edition, 2001), 457.
2. Ibid.

For Reflection & Discussion

1. How does it help your understanding of Ezekiel's vision of dry bones to see it as a reverse battle? How appropriate is it, then, to compare the violence and death resulting from a battle to peacemaking and new life in a "reverse battle"?
2. What is the meaning given to this incredible vision, as outlined in verses 11–14 of Ezekiel chapter 37?

3. How did Ezekiel's reputation ("Crazy old Zeke is at it again!") work against and sometimes for him among the exiles and those remaining in Jerusalem?

.4. The visionary experience of Ezekiel's divine calling as a prophet reveals much about the future relationship between prophet and people. What was the repeated direction given to Ezekiel? Why do you think God would repeatedly use the term "rebellious house" for the people of Judah?

5. Review Jeremiah's vision of the baskets of figs. What are the various warnings and promises in this vision?

6. Why did most people in Judah suffer from a narrow view of their national relationship with God?

7. Over time Ezekiel's prophetic calling transitioned from God's watchman among the exiles to that of "bringer of hope." What might that say about the functioning of a prophetic people in modern-day society?

8. Ezekiel singled out false prophets, bureaucratic priests, and inept national leaders as to why God had executed judgement against all of Judah? What did he say to each group and why?

9. Abraham Joshua Heschel is quoted that "the prophetic act is an encounter of a concrete person and the living God. The prophet is responsive, not only receptive. The act is often a dialogue in which consciousness of time, remembrance of events of the past, and concern with the plight of the present come into play." Compare that to the idea that a prophet is merely God's mouthpiece.

10. What are some of the social, political, economic, and spiritual ways that people can experience exile in our own day? How does the Christian message of hope tied to Jesus Christ offer a pathway to the future for these people?

Chapter 7

Jesus of Nazareth: Dueling Empires

It was a drama for the ages. Not that anybody realized it at the time.

The two men faced off against each another. One represented the greatest and most ruthless power ever created by humankind. Its military, its economic clout, and its broad social and cultural power were all brought under the reach and command of Caesar.

He alone throughout the empire was known as "Lord" and "Savior," the bringer of "peace": *pax Romana*.

The other man stood alone. Not just abandoned by the religious leaders of his own people, he was victimized by their devious plot to kill him. Penniless, powerless, and homeless, he had even been deserted by his closest friends and disciples.

Obviously, this man didn't stand a chance against the full power and weight of the Roman empire. His judge would probably forget all about him as soon as he had infamously washed his hands of yet another nuisance case among these Jews.

117

Pontius Pilate had the unenviable task of governing this troublesome outpost on the fringes of the empire: Judea, Galilee, Samaria.

Once upon a time, under David and Solomon, Israel was a kingdom to be reckoned with. But a series of weak kings and tribal squabbles led to divided northern and southern kingdoms. They had the misfortune of being caught between Egypt to the south and a succession of superpowers to the north: first Assyria, then Babylon, Persia, and Greece. Now it was Rome's turn.

Historians might well conclude these Hebrews were simply the wrong people in the wrong place at the wrong moment—time and again. Yet the Jews, the surviving remnant of Israel, held fast to the belief their God, Yahweh, was the One True God, and Jerusalem was the center of the universe.

Rome had squashed every upstart nationalistic leader and movement—and there had been a lot of them. Why should this Galilean carpenter and itinerant teacher/rabbi/miracle-worker be any different? After all, he had no army, just a few disciples and followers who had deserted him soon after his arrest. Even his closest friend, Peter, three times had denied knowing him on that fateful Thursday night.

> **"Historians might well conclude these Hebrews were simply the wrong people in the wrong place at the wrong moment—time and again."**

Two thousand years ago, hardly a soul even knew this encounter occurred, much less that it actually represented a battle of dueling empires for the ages! Who would have imagined that eventually the empire Pilate represented would crumble?

Even more remarkably, that the followers of this Galilean would not only take control of the Roman empire but extend a new religion around the planet. Its adherents would number in the billions. All that gets way ahead of our story, however.

We know about the trial of Jesus before Pontius Pilate because all four Gospel writers give us accounts. They vary in details, although the storyline is similar. Here is how the writer we know as John put it:

> Then Pilate entered the headquarters again, summoned Jesus, and asked him, "Are you the King of the Jews?" Jesus answered, "Do you ask this on your own, or did others tell you about me?"
>
> Pilate replied, "I am not a Jew, am I? Your own nation and the chief priests have handed you over to me. What have you done?"
>
> Jesus answered, "My kingdom is not from this world. If my kingdom were from this world, my followers would be fighting to keep me from being handed over to the Jews. But as it is, my kingdom is not from here."
>
> Pilate asked him, "So you are a king?"
>
> Jesus answered, "You say that I am a king. For this I was born, and for this I came into the world, to testify to the truth. Everyone who belongs to the truth listens to

my voice." Pilate asked him, "What is
truth?"   —John 18:33–38

It might appear to the casual observer that up
until this moment Jesus was just having a really bad
day. But his appearance before Pilate—and earlier
before the puppet-king Herod Antipas—was not the
result of a comedy of errors and missteps. No, this
dramatic setting came about be-cause of secret
intrigue and collusion between the Jewish temple
hierarchy and their Roman overseers.

In the bigger picture, it reflects the activity of
what Apostle Paul later would refer to as "principalities and powers." Today, many would conclude
it was part of a divine plan with cosmic and eternal
significance. Centuries of institutional traditions
and complex theologies within the Christian Church
have added layers of nuanced doctrine to explain
the what and the why of it all.

It's next to impossible to clearly separate the
teachings, ministry, and activity of "Jesus of
Nazareth" from the cosmic, eternal nature and
purpose of "Jesus the Christ" and what that means
for the salvation of humankind and creation itself.

For our purpose here, let's try at least to narrow
the scope to the prophetic activity, knowing full well
that it will include elements of both the former and
the latter Jesus.

In one sense, this confrontation between Jesus
and Pilate represented Good versus evil. Light
versus Darkness. God's power and human will. The
peaceable reign of God "on earth as it is in heaven"
and Caesar's empire of ruthless domination. That is
the lens through which we'll look at the events of a
most remarkable week.

That week had started so well, with Jesus' entry into the holy city of Jerusalem. Here's how the Gospel writer we know as Luke put it:

> [Jesus] went on ahead, going up to Jerusalem. When he had come near Bethphage and Bethany, at the place called the Mount of Olives, he sent two of the disciples, saying, "Go into the village ahead of you, and as you enter it you will find tied there a colt that has never been ridden. Untie it and bring it here. If anyone asks you, 'Why are you untying it?' just say this, 'The Lord needs it.'"
>
> So those who were sent departed and found it as he had told them. As they were untying the colt, its owners asked them, "Why are you untying the colt?" They said, "The Lord needs it." Then they brought it to Jesus; and after throwing their cloaks on the colt, they set Jesus on it.
>
> As he rode along, people kept spreading their cloaks on the road. As he was now approaching the path down from the Mount of Olives, the whole multitude of the disciples began to praise God joyfully with a loud voice for all the deeds of power that they had seen, saying, "Blessed is the king who comes in the name of the Lord! Peace in heaven, and glory in the highest heaven!"
>
> Some of the Pharisees in the crowd said to him, "Teacher, order your disciples to stop." He answered, "I tell you, if these were silent, the stones would shout out."
>
> As he came near and saw the city, he wept over it, saying, "If you, even you, had

only recognized on this day the things that
make for peace! But now they are hidden
from your eyes. Indeed, the days will come
upon you, when your enemies will set up
ramparts around you and surround you,
and hem you in on every side. They will
crush you to the ground, you and your
children within you, and they will not leave
within you one stone upon another; because
you did not recognize the time of your visi-
tatation from God."

Then he entered the temple and began to
drive out those who were selling things
there; and he said, "It is written, 'My house
shall be a house of prayer'; but you have
made it a den of robbers."

Every day he was teaching in the temple.
The chief priests, the scribes, and the leaders of the people kept looking for a way to
kill him; but they did not find anything they
could do, for all the people were spellbound
by what they heard.

—Luke 20:28–48

There's a lot going on here, not just in the Gospel
writers' narratives, but between the lines and buried
beneath the surface. There's multiple layers, filled
with literal, metaphoric, and symbolic meaning. The
story is so much bigger than a guy riding a donkey
into town while people cheer and dance around him.

Today in Christian churches all over the world,
this "happy day," Palm Sunday, is recounted by
folks who know only too well the tragedy and heart-
break to come from Thursday night into Friday.
Those first Palm Sunday celebrants had no idea
what was to come.

By the time Jesus makes his entry in Jerusalem it shouldn't come as a surprise to anybody reading the Gospels where this story is headed. This isn't just the first-century equivalent of a flash mob.

No, Jesus is entering the holy city of Jerusalem on Mount Zion to confront his destiny and the principalities and powers lined up against him. As later Christian theologians would put it, this week would mark the meridian point in *all* history.

"This isn't just the first-century equivalent of a flash mob."

For starters, there's more than passing allusion to the coronation parade of Solomon (see 1 Kings 1:32–40), who rode King David's donkey into Jerusalem amid great fanfare and accompanied by the priest Zadok and the prophet Nathan. And, of course, there is the prophet Zechariah's familiar words:

> "Rejoice greatly, O daughter Zion! Shout aloud, O daughter Jerusalem! Lo, your king comes to you; triumphant and victorious is he, humble and riding on a donkey, on a colt, the foal of a donkey. He will cut off the chariot from Ephraim and the war-horse from Jerusalem; and the battle bow shall be cut off, and he shall command peace to the nations; his dominion shall be from sea to sea, and from the River to the ends of the earth." —Zechariah 9:9–10

The Gospel writer Matthew, for his part, goes to what at first appears to be rather awkward lengths to perfectly match up Jesus' triumphant entry to

Zechariah's prophetic description, right down to having Jesus ride on a female donkey *and* its colt.

The image naturally arises for us of something like a circus entertainer entering the big top astride two matched horses. What is probably more likely is that Jesus rode the female donkey, its nursing foal tied to and following as close to its mother as possible. Luke simplifies it to a single animal. As fascinating as this speculation may be, we miss the point if all we can do is argue about donkeys, though.

Jesus' parade wasn't the only one in Jerusalem that day. It was Pilate's traditional practice at the beginning of Passover to travel the 75 miles from his Roman provincial capital in Judea, Caesarea, on the Mediterranean coast, to Jerusalem.

With the local population swelling at least ten-fold for this important Jewish holiday, Pilate wanted to keep close tabs on a potentially volatile setting. After all, there's nothing quite like a massive display of military force to intimidate would-be radicals.

Pilate rode into Jerusalem from the west on a magnificent steed. Following him were row upon row of centurions, their armor and spears glistening in the noonday sun. Dozens of chariots and soldiers on horseback complete this picture. An impressive pageant, no doubt. But the real purpose was to re-affirm, just in case anybody missed it, who was really in charge.

For all we know, that impressive parade could have been taking place across town at exactly the same time as Jesus' arrival from the east.

The differences between these two could not be more striking. The Gospel writers wrote their accounts with Solomon and Zechariah in mind. The prophet's central figure was a peacemaker who had conquered the powers-that-be and instituted his peaceable rule, extending Yahweh's dominion from sea to sea and to the ends of the earth.

Eventually, Jesus headed to the temple, whose ruling class cooperated with their Roman masters in subjugating and keeping in line the masses of people. He knew what he was doing by upsetting the moneychangers' tables and the almost-certain consequences.

Later in the week, praying mightily and alone in Gethsemene, Jesus would encapsulate his relationship with his heavenly Father: "Let this cup pass from me, but nevertheless may your will be done."

"Let this cup pass from me, but nevertheless may your will be done."

Walter Brueggemann, in *The Prophetic Imagination*, wrote: "Directed by Rome and Temple, this oppressive [Domination] System was responsible for Jesus' death and for the hunger, poverty, violence, and despair that were part of daily life for the vast majority of his contemporaries."[1]

That Domination System had a three-fold identity: (1) A politics of oppression, (2) an economics of exploitation, and (3) a religion of legitimation. In confronting that system, Jesus risked it all and prepared the way for his disciples and followers.

Two millennia later, how well have we disciples done with that? As Episcopal Bishop John Spong put it: "Most churches will die of boredom long before they die of controversy. They are unwilling to risk death in order to engage the search for truth."[2]

Many a church-goer buoyed up by triumphalism would happily jump from "Hosanna, the Messiah has come" on Palm Sunday to "Alleluia, He is risen" on Easter without having to deal with all that uncomfortable mess in between.

Nevertheless, the intervening days of Holy Week are still there. True, there are also those Christians who appear to be stuck permanently in the pain and suffering of Good Friday. Maybe that's all of life they have ever experienced. Or maybe because for them a theology of the cross explains more of reality than a theology of a risen Lord Christ.

We need both.

And so are the events of Holy Week about Jesus offering himself up as a sacrificial lamb, like a larger replaying of Abraham's attempted sacrifice of his son Isaac (only this time God went through with it)? Or was this a defiant act against not only Rome's imperial power but the oppressive, hate-filled, violence-fueled principalities and powers of all eras?

Theologians and regular church-goers will debate that for some time to come, making their appeals to scripture, tradition, and experience. Don't expect that controversy to be settled any time soon.

"Let's start from this point: Jesus was not killed by God's hand."

Let's start from this point: Jesus was not killed by God's hand. Maybe there could have been another way, but that's not how it turned out. Jesus was executed as an enemy of the state, after some of his own people (the "rulers of the Temple") connived against him. Jesus was a threat to the established order, to "the system," if you will.

The kingdom, or reign, that Jesus preached about throughout his earthly ministry was diametrically opposed to the way things were at the time. He taught his disciples to turn the other cheek, to go the extra mile, to repay violence with kindness. The last would be first and the first would be last. Give to Caesar the things that belong to Caesar but give to God what belongs to God. Jesus' idea of "suffering servanthood" drew directly on the prophetic imagery from Isaiah. Read through the Beatitudes in Matthew chapter 5 and you will find the antithesis of how worldly powers operate.

It's not just the Gospel writers whose voices need to be heard in this discussion. Apostle Paul would be responsible for giving much of the shape, character, and vision to the emerging Christian fellowship.

Noted Anglican scholar and bishop N. T. Wright helps to put Paul's message in the context of the political and social world of its time:

> Paul was not opposed to Caesar's empire because it was an empire, with all the unpleasant things we have learned to associate with that word, but because it was Caesar's, and because Caesar was claiming divine status and honors which belonged only to the one God.[3]

Even before Jesus was born, it was clear that his life would be different, that in ways large and small he would confront the status quo. *That is the role of a prophet!* Yes, in time he would come to be known as Lord and Savior, Messiah (in Greek, Christ).

Remember the song attributed to his mother Mary, sung in response to an angel bearing incredible news:

And Mary said, "My soul magnifies the Lord, and my spirit rejoices in God my Savior, for he has looked with favor on the lowliness of his servant. Surely, from now on all generations will call me blessed; for the Mighty One has done great things for me, and holy is his name. His mercy is for those who fear him from generation to generation. He has shown strength with his arm; he has scattered the proud in the thoughts of their hearts. He has brought down the powerful from their thrones, and lifted up the lowly; he has filled the hungry with good things, and sent the rich away empty. He has helped his servant Israel, in remembrance of his mercy, according to the promise he made to our ancestors, to Abraham and to his descendants forever."

—Luke 1:46–55

All this and more explains how Jesus ended up standing before Pontius Pilate, offering these words: "For this I was born, and for this I came into the world, to testify to the truth. Everyone who belongs to the truth listens to my voice."

Pilate had no understanding of Truth. **Jesus was not only speaking truth to power; he *was* (and *is*) Truth!**

Standing before Pilate, Jesus was not simply confronting Roman authority. He was confronting injustice and idolatry, hubris and greed, the source of violence and pain and misery, the very personification of everything that stood in the way of establishing God's reign of peace on earth as it is in heaven.

Notes

1. Walter Brueggemann, *The Prophetic Imagination* (Philadelphia: Fortress Press, 1978), chapter 1.
2. John Spong, *A New Christianity for a New World: Why Traditional Faith Is Dying and How a New Faith Is Being Born* (New York: HarperCollins, 1st ed. Paperpack edition, 2002), 125.
3. N. T. Wright, "Paul's Gospel and Caesar's Empire," in Richard A. Horsley, ed., *Paul and Politics: Essays in Honor of Krister Stendahl* (Harrisburg, Pennsylvania: Trinity Press International, 2000), 164.

For Reflection & Discussion

1. Why is it so difficult to focus just on the prophetic nature of Jesus' ministry? Is it even possible for Christians to separate into different categories his roles as prophet and teacher, Lord and Savior, Son of God, Cosmic Christ, and the second member of the Triune Godhead?
2. Why was Jesus on trial before Pontius Pilate? What were the stated charges against the state (Caesar) and some of the underlying issues?
3. Read aloud the description in John 18 of Jesus' trial. Why do you think Jesus and Pilate were having trouble communicating on the same plane of understanding?
4. The author compares the interaction between Jesus and Pilate at his trial with the much different events at the beginning of that week. What are some of the multiple layers of literal and literary meaning going on in this account? Why was it so important to Gospel writers to tie Jesus to Old Testament figures?

5. How was Jesus acting like a prophet when he upset the moneychangers' tables in the Temple?

6. What do you think of Walter Brueggeman's claim: "Directed by Rome and Temple, this oppressive [Domination] System was responsible for Jesus' death and for the hunger, poverty, violence, and despair that were part of daily life for the vast majority of his contemporaries"?

7. The events of Holy Week can be understood as Jesus offering himself up as a sacrificial lamb (something akin to Abraham's "almost sacrifice" of his son Isaac) or as defiant acts against not only Rome's imperial power but the oppressive, hate-filled, violence-fueled principalities and powers of all eras. Discuss the implications of each alternative. Which position appeals to you the most? Why?

8. Read Mary's song recorded in Luke 1:46–55 (sometimes referred to as the Magnificat), which was her response to the angel's message. In what ways does this reflect a prophetic message?

9. Face to face with Caesar's representative, Jesus spoke truth to power: "For this I was born, and for this I came into the world, to testify to the truth. Everyone who belongs to the truth listens to my voice." What is the message here for a modern-day prophetic people?

Chapter 8

Paul of Tarsus: Expanding God's Family

Let's begin with the obvious question: *What is Apostle Paul doing here in this study of ancient Hebrew prophets?*

Sure, a case can be made for including Jesus of Nazareth: He was, after all, a Jew and remained one his whole life. But isn't Paul (even when you consider he started out as Saul, an observant Jew who was schooled in the tradition of the Pharisees) best remembered as Christianity's first great convert, church planter, and theologian? Didn't he leave behind his Jewish identity after the dramatic experience of his conversion on the road to Damascus?

Actually, no, he did not.

In his own writings Paul gave no indication whatsoever that he turned away from Judaism to become a Christian. And as for that experience on the way to Damascus—a significant number of scholars (both Jewish and Christian, by the way) view it as a *call* not a *conversion.*[1]

A close look at accounts of that experience, in Paul's words found in Galatians 1:13–16 and by the

131

writer of Acts (in 9:1–19, 22:6–16, and 26:12–18) show a strong resemblance to the calling of ancient Hebrew prophets, particularly Isaiah, Jeremiah, and Ezekiel.

> ## *"In his own writings Paul gave no indication whatsoever that he turned away from Judaism to "become" a Christian."*

Look at the way those prophets received their callings: chosen by God even before birth (Isaiah 49:1), surrounded by light as the Lord spoke (Ezekiel 1:28), and given a specific commission (Jeremiah 1:7). Paul's experience places him clearly within this prophetic tradition.

Furthermore, what Paul is to accomplish for the Gentiles is a reflection of the prophecies that the eyes of the blind shall be opened and that salvation will come:

> ...to open their eyes so that they may turn from darkness to light and from the power of Satan to God, so that they may receive forgiveness of sins and a place among those who are sanctified by faith in [Christ].
> —Acts 26:18

> Then the eyes of the blind shall be opened, and the ears of the deaf unstopped.
> —Isaiah 35:5

> I have given you as a covenant to the people, a light to the nations, to open the eyes that are blind, to bring out the prisoners from the dungeon, from the prison those who sit

in darkness.... I will lead the blind by a road they do not know, by paths they have not known I will guide them. —Isaiah 42:7, 16

The Spirit of the Lord God is upon me, because the Lord has anointed me; he has sent me to bring good news to the oppressed, to bind up the brokenhearted, to proclaim liberty to the captives, and release to the prisoners. —Isaiah 61:1

Krister Stendahl, one of the most respected Christian scholars of Paul, wrote:

Again and again we find that there is hardly a thought of Paul's which is not tied up with his mission, with his work. The 'I' in his writings is not 'the Christian' but 'the Apostle to the Gentiles.' That is why I say call rather than conversion."[2]

Paul's mission, his life's work, was to expand the boundaries of the chosen "Family of God" to include Gentiles alongside the Jews. The experience on the Damascus Road was simply the opening act in a long process of commissioning Paul as apostle to the Gentiles (by authority of the risen Lord Jesus!).

Scriptural accounts show that after spending a short time in Damascus (instructed by Ananias) Paul briefly returned to Jerusalem before heading off to "the wilderness" for several years of spiritual preparation.

Once again, note the similarity to the way ancient prophets spent time in the wilderness preparing for their mission. Of course, the same is true for both Jesus and John the Baptist.

It is often assumed, as well, that the spectacular Damascus Road experience was also the moment he changed his name from the Jewish/Hebraic Saul to the Greek Paul.

Unfortunately, he never gives us a clue about this issue in his own letters. But Luke does in Acts, although indirectly. He uses the name Saul exclusively up to chapter 13, where the expression "Saul, also known as Paul" is used in verse 9. From that moment on the apostle is referred to only as Paul.

What's going on in chapter 13?

Saul was on the island of Cyprus, along with his traveling companions Barnabas and John. While they were there a magician (described as a "Jewish false prophet") attempted to turn the Roman proconsul Sergius Paulus against Saul and his teachings about Jesus Christ.

When "Saul, also known as Paul" blinded the magician by the power of the Holy Spirit, the proconsul was "astonished at the teaching about the Lord" and believed. Afterward Paul and his companions set sail for Perga, where John left them and returned to Jerusalem. Paul and Barnabas headed for Antioch.

The symbolism here is important: Instead of returning to Jerusalem and dealing once again with leaders of the Jewish-Christian community, Paul began to turn his attention away from Jerusalem and toward his ultimate goal of reaching Rome and, he hoped, to the barbarians beyond (beginning with what we know as Spain). His acceptance of a mission to take the good news of Christ to the Gentiles was now complete.

Just because Paul had a clear vision of his mission didn't guarantee its success or even that he would be received well—both then and now.

Mark Nanos, a foremost Jewish authority on Paul, has noted,

> It is no small wonder that this Paul is not well liked. Jews often perceive him as a traitor, or worse. Christians often consider him arrogant and manipulative, at the very least, and among scholars and those sensitive to the integrity of Jews and Judaism his perceived disregard for and betrayal of his Jewish heritage and the Jewish people is justifiable cause for suspicion.[3]

Paul's primary concern, of course, definitely was not popularity. In almost euphoric language he described to the church in Philippi the transforming result of knowing Christ:

> Yet whatever gains I had, these I have come to regard as loss because of Christ. More than that, I regard everything as loss because of the surpassing value of knowing Christ Jesus my Lord.
>
> For his sake I have suffered the loss of all things, and I regard them as rubbish, in order that I may gain Christ and be found in him, not having a righteousness of my own that comes from the law, but one that comes through the faith of Christ, the righteousness from God based on faith.
>
> I want to know Christ and the power of his resurrection and the sharing of his sufferings by becoming like him in his death, if somehow I may attain the resurrection from the dead.

> Not that I have already obtained this or
> have already reached the goal; but I press
> on to make it my own, because Christ Jesus
> has made me his own. —Philippians 3:7–12

This transformation is, first of all, about relationships: with God through Jesus Christ and then with
his fellow believers. That is what connects him in a
special way to his Hebraic ancestors beginning with
Abraham and continuing through the prophets. In
turn, it seeks to answer the question of what it
means to be God's people, or family.

Recall all of the family-related metaphors used by
the prophet Hosea (see chapter 4 in this text). Yet
Paul was not simply content to restate ancient understandings and truths. He extended and expanded
them. His inclusiveness reflected a respect for all
individuals without consideration of age, gender,
social standing, or economic status:

> As many of you as were baptized into Christ
> have clothed yourselves with Christ. There
> is no longer Jew or Greek, there is no longer
> slave or free, there is no longer male and
> female; for all of you are one in Christ
> Jesus. And if you belong to Christ, then you
> are Abraham's offspring, heirs according to
> the promise. —Galatians 3:27–29

> Consider your own call, brothers and
> sisters: not many of you were wise by
> human standards, not many were powerful,
> not many were of noble birth. But God
> chose what is foolish in the world to shame
> the wise; God chose what is weak in the
> world to shame the strong; God chose what

is low and despised in the world, things that are not, to reduce to nothing things that are, so that no one might boast in the presence of God. He is the source of your life in Christ Jesus, who became for us wisdom from God, and righteousness and sanctification and redemption, in order that, as it is written, "Let the one who boasts, boast in the Lord."
　　　　　—1 Corinthians 1:26–31

For just as the body is one and has many members, and all the members of the body, though many, are one body, so it is with Christ. For in the one Spirit we were all baptized into one body—Jews or Greeks, slaves or free—and we were all made to drink of one Spirit. Indeed, the body does not consist of one member but of many.
　　　　　—1 Corinthians 12:12–14

One challenge we face today when reading the letters attributed to Paul in the New Testament is assuming that they were all actually written by him because his name is attached. This is one of those areas for dispute among biblical scholars and devoted readers.

There is near universal agreement that at least seven of the letters are authentic: Romans, 1 and 2 Corinthians, Galatians, Philippians, 1 Thessalonians, and Philemon.

Many scholars believe the Pastoral letters (1 and 2 Timothy and Titus) and 2 Thessalonians were probably written long after Paul's death, which occurred sometime around 70 CE. Those four books are sometimes referred to as "Post-Pauline."

The two remaining letters, Ephesians and
Colossians, stir the most controversy. They are so
similar that whoever wrote one probably wrote the
other, perhaps a close associate of Paul's. They are
referred to as "pseudo-Pauline."

"There is near universal agreement that at least seven of the letters are authentic."

The content of the letters, moving from authentic
Pauline to pseudo-Pauline to post-Pauline shows
first a development in the increasingly institutional
Christian fellowship. We see a gradual movement
from function to institutional form (for example,
from "serving" to the specific office of deacon). They
also evidence a changing stance regarding the role
of women in the church.

The concluding chapter in Romans mentions
several women who played prominent roles in the
church alongside Paul.

There is "our sister Phoebe, a deacon of the
church at Cenchreae," who is described also as "a
benefactor of many and of myself as well" (Romans
16:1–2). Paul mentions women named Mary, "who
has worked very hard among you" (16:6), Julia, and
the unnamed sister of Nercus (16:15).

Here in Romans, as well as other letters, Paul
gives thanks for a husband-wife team, Aquila and
Prisca (Priscilla) who opened their home to be used
as a gathering spot for the believers:

Greet Prisca and Aquila, who work with me
in Christ Jesus, and who risked their necks

for my life, to whom not only I give thanks
but also all the churches of the Gentiles.
Greet also the church in their house.
        —Romans 16:3–5

Probably the most interesting reference to a
woman comes in verse 7: "Greet Andronicus and
Junia, my compatriots who were in prison with me;
they are prominent among the apostles, and they
were in Christ before I was."

Centuries later, scribes copying this letter
concluded that it was impossible for a woman to
have served as an apostle at any time in the church.
They changed the spelling of Junia to what would be
in Greek the masculine form of the name. However,
no such name (Junias) has ever been found in contemporary Greek literature or correspondence.

A growing rigidity can be observed in counsel
regarding women in the Christian fellowship. In
chapter 11 of 1 Corinthians, a passage regarded as
"authentically Paul," direction is given that a man
who prays or prophecies with something on his
head is a disgrace.

Likewise, a woman who prays or prophesies with
her head unveiled is a disgrace. The key element in
this is not whether a head is veiled or unveiled. It's
clear that both men and women were praying and
prophesying.

Compare that to passages in Ephesians 5 and
Colossians 3 (considered pseudo-Pauline), the
Pastorals (1 Timothy chapters 2, 4, and 5; 2 Timothy
3; and Titus), and 1 Corinthians 14 (which many
scholars contend was added much later by another
author and should be considered post-Pauline, as
well).

Wives, be subject to your husbands as you
are to the Lord. For the husband is the head
of the wife just as Christ is the head of the
church, the body of which he is the Savior.
Just as the church is subject to Christ, so
also wives ought to be, in everything, to
their husbands. —Ephesians 5:22-24

Wives, be subject to your husbands, as is
fitting in the Lord. Husbands, love your
wives and never treat them harshly.
Children, obey your parents in everything,
for this is your acceptable duty in the Lord.
Fathers, do not provoke your children, or
they may lose heart. Slaves, obey your
earthly masters in everything, not only
while being watched and in order to please
them, but wholeheartedly, fearing the Lord.
                        —Colossians 3:18–22

Counsel regarding women eventually took on an
even stricter tone. Note, in particular, how the
example of Eve is brought into the discussion. She is
identified as the one who succumbed to temptation
and brought condemnation on Adam—*and, in turn,
on all men!*

Let a woman learn in silence with full
submission. I permit no woman to teach or
to have authority over a man; she is to keep
silent. For Adam was formed first, then Eve;
and Adam was not deceived, but the woman
was deceived and became a transgressor.
Yet she will be saved through childbearing,
provided they continue in faith and love and
holiness, with modesty. —1 Timothy 2:11–15

Let a widow be put on the list if she is not less than sixty years old and has been married only once; she must be well attested for her good works, as one who has brought up children, shown hospitality, washed the saints' feet, helped the afflicted, and devoted herself to doing good in every way.

But refuse to put younger widows on the list; for when their sensual desires alienate them from Christ, they want to marry, and so they incur condemnation for having violated their first pledge. Besides that, they learn to be idle, gadding about from house to house; and they are not merely idle, but also gossips and busybodies, saying what they should not say.

So I would have younger widows marry, bear children, and manage their households, so as to give the adversary no occasion to revile us. —1 Timothy 5:9–14

You must understand this, that in the last days distressing times will come. For people will be lovers of themselves, lovers of money, boasters, arrogant, abusive, disobedient to their parents, ungrateful, unholy, inhuman, implacable, slanderers, profligates, brutes, haters of good, treacherous, reckless, swollen with conceit, lovers of pleasure rather than lovers of God, holding to the outward form of godliness but denying its power. Avoid them!

For among them are those who make their way into households and captivate silly women, overwhelmed by their sins and

swayed by all kinds of desires, who are always being instructed and can never arrive at a knowledge of the truth.
—2 Timothy 3:1–7

Likewise, tell the older women to be reverent in behavior, not to be slanderers or slaves to drink; they are to teach what is good, so that they may encourage the young women to love their husbands, to love their children, to be self-controlled, chaste, good managers of the household, kind, being submissive to their husbands, so that the word of God may not be discredited.
—Titus 2:3–5

A more comprehensive study of how the early Christian communities developed into institutional churches and, ultimately, an "orthodox" church is beyond the scope of this book. But it should be plain to see that the Christian church did not attain its ultimate shape, character, and mission immediately.

Many factors were at work, not least of which was its evolving relationship with the surrounding culture and the Roman empire itself.

Inevitably, of course, expansion of the Family of God—whether by race, gender, national origin, language, or orientation—leads to a multiverse.

In the early years of the 21st century, Christianity now offers an often bewildering choice of orthodoxies (multiple "right ways" of thinking) and orthopraxis (an equally numerous array of "right practices").

Every tradition, sect, denomination, and group appears to have its own orthodoxy and orthopraxis. Sooner or later Apostle Paul's name crops up in just about everybody's attempts to justify their doctrines and practices. Yet where is Truth in it all?

"Every tradition, sect, denomination, and group appears to have its own orthodoxy and orthopraxis."

A core consideration for the idea of a prophetic people in the 21st century is finding a way for all those various voices within an expanded family of God to not only be heard but to be part of the decision-making function of the church. One answer may be found within a new and somewhat unwieldy term: **Orthoparadoxy.**

Here's what Dwight J. Friesen has to say about this:

> The ministry of God's people has always been understood as a ministry of blessing—from God's call to Abraham, with the promise that Abraham and his descendants would be a blessing to the nations, to Paul's charge to the church in Corinth: "All this is from God, who reconciled us to himself through Christ and gave us the ministry of reconciliation" (2 Corinthians 5:18).
>
> Orthoparadoxy is an effort to make God's main thing the main thing for all the people of God: reconciliation. Not sameness or agreement but differentiated oneness—where the fullness of one can be in relationship with the fullness of another.
>
> Orthoparadox is right paradox—holding difference rightly. Orthoparadox seeks to hold difference, tensions, otherness, and

paradoxes with grace, humility, respect, and curiosity, while simultaneously bringing the fullness of self to the "other" in conversation, not to convert or to convince but with the hope of mutual transformation through interpersonal relationship.[4]

How beautifully this corresponds with Paul's classic statement: "Bear one another's burdens, and in this way you will fulfill the law of Christ" (Galatians 6:2). Paul became, by the transforming power of God in Christ, a new person. And that is what the "good news," the gospel, is about.

It's *not* about accepting a list of belief statements or theological doctrines. Nor is it about performing the right rituals correctly. It isn't the creation or end result of implementing successful programs or methods. There's no guarantee of a happy life or a glorious mansion in heaven after you die.

It *is* about being transformed from an old way of thinking and doing and being to living in community as faithful disciples of the One who calls us into a new and glorious life. Those faithful disciples will not all look, act, or think alike. But they're "family," God's family, and that is what makes all the difference.

Notes

1. For an excellent introduction to the New Perspective on Paul (including bibliography of books and scholarly papers), see *www.thepaulpage.com*. It also contains references to "Paul and Empire" and "Paul within Judaism."

2. Krister Stendahl, "Call Rather Than Conversion," in *Paul Among the Jews and Gentiles*, (Minneapolis, Minnesota: Fortress Press, 1976), 12.
3. Mark Nanos, *The Mystery of Romans: The Jewish Context of Paul's Letter* (Minneapolis, Minnesota: Fortress Press, 1996), 7.
4. Dwight J. Friesen, *An Emerging Manifesto of Hope* (Grand Rapids, Michigan: Baker Books/Emergent Village, 2007), 204–205.

For Reflection & Discussion

1. How does it change Paul's mission and ministry to understand his core experience as a prophetic call rather than a religious conversion?
2. What purpose does "wilderness preparation" serve for prophets? How can that find expression in prophetic communities?
3. What was the symbolic importance of Paul turning his attention away from Jerusalem and toward Rome? How can "Jerusalem" and "Rome" be expressed in your own congregational and secular settings?
4. Paul was apparently not concerned with being popular. What was he concerned about? List your congregation's top five concerns currently and what you'd like them to be in five years.
5. How is Paul's notion of inclusiveness expressed in Galatians 3:27–29, 1 Corinthians 1:26–31, and 1 Corinthians 12:12–14? Update those scripture passages for a 21st-century context.
6. Many scholars divide the letters attributed to Paul into authentic, pseudo-, and post-Pauline categories. How might this affect how you would read and use these scriptures today?

7. Discuss the varying attitudes toward women found throughout all the letters attributed to Paul. How do you account for such a wide divergence?
8. What does the author mean by using the term "orthoparadoxy"? Discuss the idea of "differentiated oneness." When have you experienced that and what was the result? How does it relate to bearing one another's burdens?

Afterword
Taking the Next Steps

The Book of Proverbs includes this bit of basic wisdom: "Where there is no vision, the people perish."

Sometimes we leave the "vision thing"[1] to academics, to the scholars and theologians who appear to care the most about philosophical underpinnings. Or maybe that apparently unpleasant task is handed off to the kind of folks who love developing five- or ten-year action plans. The rest of us generally find reasons why we're too busy to engage in the process.

All too often, Christianity has substituted creeds and basic-belief statements for prophetic vision. The institutional nature of the church practically demands that. There must be a clear line between who is in (orthodoxy) and who is not (heresy).

Prophets make very poor gatekeepers or pastors. They're provokers and troublemakers. Make a line in the sand in front of them and they'll cross it just about every time.

That being said, you wouldn't want a church of just prophets, either. That's why being a prophetic community is a challenging, often dangerous undertaking. When does transformation cross over into self-destruction?

147

Beliefs matter, though. They offer substance and depth. But they're not the starting point for communities of prophetic disciples seeking to rediscover the Way of Jesus. That's where principles come in, because they can offer direction without necessarily erecting rigid boundaries.

A few years ago my denomination, Community of Christ, introduced a list of nine principles.[2] Not everyone in the church probably realized at the time how critical that was.

I had worked for more than 20 years as a book and magazine editor for the denomination and its publishing house. One of the many book projects I'd worked on was a major revision of the book titled *Basic Beliefs*. Previous versions of that core reference work had guided leaders and members for many decades.

The book is, I believe, still available and used, although it has lost prominence to newer resource materials emphasizing these enduring principles:

- Grace and Generosity
- Sacredness of Creation
- Continuing Revelation
- Worth of All Persons
- All Are Called
- Responsible Choices
- Pursuit of Peace (Shalom)
- Unity in Diversity
- Blessings of Community

My faith community is far from unique in doing something like this. Our list of enduring principles has a lot to do with our particular history, theology, tradition, and visionary outlook. Other churches have their own lists, developed for much the same kinds of reasons. There would undoubtedly be both overlap and disjuncture comparing lists. That's not my point, however.

What matters is that **principles ought to come first**. They have a way of stimulating thinking and producing ideas that eventually lead to action. And for prophetic communities, it's action guided by the Holy Spirit that matters.

"Prophets make very poor gatekeepers or pastors. They're provokers and troublemakers."

The African-American abolitionist Frederick Douglass, who had been born into slavery in Maryland, put it this way in his autobiography: "I prayed for freedom for twenty years but received no answer until I prayed with my legs."[3]

As an example of how this process can work within a faith community, let me tell you a story about my own congregation. It's just one of many stories I could tell, but I'm most familiar with this one.

Some years ago a top denominational executive came to my congregation. In the course of her remarks, she commented that it was a *good* congregation, but not a *great* one. Folks were polite enough not to tell her what they might have thought of her comments. But I could sense there was a bit of an undercurrent to their outward graciousness.

I don't recall how much detail she offered to support her critique. Still, I had a good idea what she was getting at. Ours was a busy church with a large, active youth program. There were Sunday school classes for children, teenagers, and adults. Worship services regularly featured talented musicians and public speakers. We were pretty good at meeting both pastoral and social needs of the membership.

> ### *Like many local churches, regardless of denominational affiliation, my congregation was focused on maintaining its "busyness."*

Although it had only been around since the early 1980s, the congregation had grown larger than many others in the denomination nearby. It was financially secure, thanks to the generous support of many families. The church fit in well in its location: a growing, comfortable, middle-class suburb about 20 miles from downtown Kansas City, Missouri. The building was located on a busy highway at the rapidly expanding edge of town.

Like many local churches, regardless of denominational affiliation, my congregation was focused on maintaining its "busyness." There wasn't a great deal of outreach. Sure, we kept the doors open and warmly welcomed anyone who came to visit.

It's not that many members didn't want to reach out to the community; we just didn't really know how to take the first steps. Besides, we were attracting families already within our denomination because we were blessed with lots of children.

Fast forward to today and a different picture begins to emerge. We still offer uplifting worship and church school classes on Sunday morning. And there's active youth programs.

Now there's something else going on, too. Twice a month a different crew of about a dozen church members gathers at the church building for what we call the Necessities Pantry. We supply about 60 to 80 families with diapers, toilet paper, laundry and dishwashing detergent, and toiletries such as toothpaste and brushes, deodorant, shaving supplies, and soap. Basically, it's the items people need but can't buy with food stamps.

These families get itemized vouchers from the Community Services League (CSL), which assures need and eligibility. Instead of lining people up and handing out sacks of items, we have counselors sit down with them to talk about what's going on in their life. We want to see if we can help with other concerns or at least direct them to social-service agencies.

We soon discovered many folks burdened with ultra-high-interest loans from payday or title loan offices. It's not uncommon to find people paying interest rates somewhere in the range of 200 to 400 percent while having to continually roll over short-term loans into new ones. It's a cycle they probably can never escape on their own.

One congregation member happens to be president of a Catholic credit union in Kansas City. Others volunteer regularly with CSL. That led to a joint effort to help people get out from under this predatory loan trap. They may now be able to pay off their high-interest loans and replace them with far more reasonably priced credit union loans.

We also realized that some of the people we were helping at the pantry couldn't get a job because they didn't own a car. That's essential in our part of the county where there is no public transportation at all. This led to contacting an auto dealership in a nearby town.

Many of the older cars they were getting on trade-ins weren't quite new enough for their own used-car lot. Typically, those cars were sent to an auto auction. Now, however, some are repaired and offered for sale at a reasonable price using credit union/CSL loans. Several congregation members also teach a money-management class sponsored by CSL at local libraries.

While the congregation was moving out in these areas, we became aware of an interfaith program called Open Table.[4] As a year-long effort, about a dozen individuals assist a "brother or sister" to find adequate housing, employment, education, and an array of necessary social skills.

I relate these efforts not to brag about my congregation. Honestly, I'm still not sure I'd classify the congregation as "great," although I find that kind of thing less helpful these days anyway. Besides, congregations both small and big can be found engaging in these kinds of ministries and much more.

My point here, though, is to show how we got from Point A years ago to Point B today. It wasn't a straight line. Nor was it a one-way street. We are being transformed bit by bit as we open ourselves to others and their needs.

There was no detailed five- or ten-year plan. Not that there's anything wrong with those, mind you. I've seen them work elsewhere. It just wasn't how it worked with us. Rather, one individual a few years back persisted in raising the idea of a necessities pantry after seeing how one worked in a neighboring city. Clearly, there was a need in our own part of the county.

Other church members joined in the effort, contacts were made with CSL, a small line item was added to the congregational budget, and we even got a seed-money grant from our denomination.

Several months later we opened the pantry for the first time. Each month a few more people came, and we've begun to develop a relationship with some of them.

Then the idea of an alternative to payday/title loans was raised. That, in turn, led to the used-car loan program. Eventually all this led to lobbying of city councils to restrict the number of payday loan offices. Recently, one of those councils capped the number of such lenders so that when one closes it cannot be replaced by another.

The plan is simple: somebody gets an idea, others join to help develop it and make it a reality. Then that leads to another idea and another and another. As the old saying goes, this isn't rocket science. But it is one way a prophetic community brings change and transformation. Who knows where it will lead?

"The plan is simple: somebody gets an idea, others join to help develop it and make it a reality."

In our case, I think something else has been going on. I trace it back to a cold January Sunday evening in 2003. We had no way of knowing then that the tragedy that unfolded that night might lead to eventual blessings.

That night a man broke into our church building, apparently looking for money to support what we later learned was an alcohol and gambling addiction. He didn't find any cash lying around, but for reasons still unclear, he lit some candles.

Fire-department investigators couldn't definitely say if an accelerant had been used. But the end result was that almost the entire interior of the building was gutted. Fortunately, the fire didn't burn through the exterior.

We wouldn't move back in until Christmas. Another congregation a few miles away graciously welcomed us. We held early worship during their Sunday-school hour, then reversed the order.

A huge number of decisions had to be made, beginning with taking inventory of what had been lost. We met with countless insurance claims adjusters, various city and fire-district inspectors, denominational and mid-level church officials, architects, engineers, contractors, and subcontractors. But this turned out to be the most critical question of all: *Do we want to return and rebuild?*

One option was to merge our congregation with the one whose building we were sharing. There also were some hints from the Methodists next door to our original site they might be interested in buying the property. If we used sale and insurance money, should we buy land to build a new structure or purchase a vacant church building?

All of this complicated what I call our **exile experience.** In the end, we unanimously decided to return and rebuild. We remembered how our congregation came into being some 25 years before when a very large congregation was split in two.

For a while the two groups shared the building, but that proved unusually stressful. Some of the problem related to the conservative/liberal or traditionalist/progressive tension roiling our denomination at the time.

Eventually a decision was reached: One group would keep the building and everything in it. Our congregation was tasked with raising funds and securing a denominational loan, finding a site, and erecting a new building. When we held our first worship service on Christmas Day 1988, it represented the conclusion of our **exodus experience.**

It's probably not wise to proclaim with absolute certainty that the Holy Spirit did this and that and other things, thereby leading to such-and-such an outcome. Yet with hindsight that may, in fact, be close to the case.

A prophetic community is not one that simply engages in worthwhile activity, doing good things to help people in need. **Beneath and behind it all there must be the movement of the Spirit that empowers and enlightens and guides.** This calls for a people with a solid spiritual foundation.

Throughout this book I have frequently relied on the words of Rabbi Abraham Joshua Heschel, whose landmark book, *The Prophets*, continues to provide the greatest, most thorough examination of the Hebrew prophets anywhere. He relates the following:

> The prophets tell us little of how the divine word came to them or how they knew it to be the word of the very God. Perhaps it was the discovery of being present at a divine event, "of standing at the council of the Lord" that was the essence of their experience and the source of evidence. **Prophetic inspiration involved participation, not merely receptivity to communication.** [*Emphasis added.*]5

155

That's the key word, *participation*. The ancient prophets didn't speak truth to power from mountaintops. They were part of the daily life of the people. That's where they were angered by the injustice, inequity, and idolatry of society. It's no different today.

Prophetic communities cannot be separate enclaves removed from reality. Although injustice, inequity, and idolatry will be expressed in different ways in 21st-century Western society, they still stand in opposition to the "mind and will of God." Apostle Paul famously counseled the Galatian church to "bear one another's burdens." That remains as a core understanding for the church in society today.

There is no one right way to become and develop as a prophetic community. Nor are there "Ten Easy Steps" that will guarantee transformative results.

The examples presented here of ancient Hebrews just scratch the surface of prophetic ministry. Those ancient prophets spoke and acted within the context of their own time and culture. That helps explain why their examples may not transfer directly or easily to today.

Western Christianity, particularly in North America in the opening decades of the 21st century, is at a crossroads. Much of the church has become focused on an individual's interior relationship with God. That has often led to a desire to simply escape this world to dwell happily in another after death. The interim is viewed as a time merely to endure hardship and suffering because nothing really can be done about it.

Prophetic Christian communities share a much different vision of the "kingdom of God on earth as it is in heaven." They are always open to how the

Holy Spirit can transform the things of this world into Christ's emerging peaceable reign.

Those aren't just fancy religious terms we throw around on Sunday mornings within the safe confines of our church buildings. They are a call to action.

There is no one right way to become and develop as a prophetic community. Nor are there "Ten Easy Steps" that will guarantee transformative results.

Just put this in the starkest of terms: There is Caesar's empire and there is God's. Which one do we serve? Which one guides our life choices? Which one will lead to an abundant life and which one will not?

The answers to those questions most likely will come not with grand spectacles like that of Elijah and the priests of Baal. They are far more likely to remind us of Elijah hiding in a mountainside cave. That's where a still, small voice urged him back to action: *"Elijah, what are you doing here?"*

That Voice asks the same question of us today.

Notes

1. This term was made famous by then-Vice President George H.W. Bush when running for President in 1987, in an interview in *Time* magazine.
2. Enduring Principles of Community of Christ; see *www.CofChrist.org/enduringprinciples.*
3. Frederick Douglass, *Narrative of the Life of Frederick Douglass* (Boston: The Anti-Slavery Office, 1845; Dover edition, 1995), 134.

4. For more information on Open Table, see *www.theopentable.net.*
5. Abraham Joshua Heschel, *The Prophets* (New York: Harper & Row, 1962; Perennial Classics Edition, 2001), 555.

For Reflection & Discussion

1. Which of the nine principles listed at the beginning speaks most directly to you? Are there others you would add to this list?
2. If you have time, write a short description of each of those principles. This could be done in pairs or small groups. Share those descriptions with others and discuss.
3. What's so important about action that is guided by the Holy Spirit? What role does individual and group spiritual direction play in a prophetic community?
4. The author gives an example of his own congregation in which one idea led to another and then to another. How often have you witnessed this kind of process?
5. What do you take from the Abraham Joshua Heschel quote that "prophetic inspiration involved participation, not merely receptivity to communication"? How true has that been in your own experiences and that of others in your faith community?
6. What are some of the basic lessons you'll take from having studied this book? How has it changed or reinforced your thinking and perspectives?
7. Which of the prophets presented here speak most directly to you today? Why?

8. What are some of the most pressing problems a contemporary prophetic people should address?
9. If you were to recommend this book to another individual or group, what advice would you give?

About the Author

A lifelong desire to know more about scripture led Richard A. Brown to Vancouver School of Theology in 1978. In Professor Lloyd Gaston's classroom, he first encountered ideas that came to be identified with the New Perspective on Paul. His time at VST would impact him throughout his life and career.

Rich went on to complete a master's degree in religion from the Park University Graduate School of Religion (a program now part of Community of Christ Seminary at Graceland University). Years before, he earned an undergraduate degree from the University of Missouri School of Journalism. He began his career as a newspaper reporter in North and West Vancouver, British Columbia.

That background was put to good use during his 23 years as an editor for Herald Publishing House and at Community of Christ International Headquarters in Independence, Missouri. As copy editor, then senior editor, he edited books as well as several journals and magazines. Eventually, he became managing editor of the *Herald*, the denomination's monthly magazine.

Rich wrote a half dozen Herald House books in the 1980s and 1990s, including a widely used study guide for adults, *Studies in Romans, Volumes 1 & 2*, and was a frequent contributor to both church and independent journals.

When his job as *Herald* editor was eliminated because of a budget crisis, Rich accepted early retirement. He created Isaac's Press and a year later published *What Was Paul Thinking?* (2010).

Rich and his wife Sally have two grown children and one grandchild.